THE ANTI-CHINESE MOVEMENT IN CALIFORNIA

THE ANTI-CHINESE MOVEMENT
IN CALIFORNIA

ELMER CLARENCE SANDMEYER

Foreword and Supplementary Bibliographies
by Roger Daniels

UNIVERSITY OF ILLINOIS PRESS
Urbana and Chicago

Illini Books edition, 1991
© 1973, 1991 by the Board of Trustees of the University of Illinois
Originally published in a clothbound edition, 1939. ISBN 0-252-00338-1.
Manufactured in the United States of America

P 5 4 3 2 1

This book is printed on acid-free paper.

Library of Congress Cataloging-in-Publication Data

Sandmeyer, Elmer Clarence, 1888–1971.
  The anti-Chinese movement in California / Elmer Clarence Sandmeyer;
  foreword and supplementary bibliographies by Roger Daniels. —
Illini Books ed.
      p.   cm.
  Enlargement of 1973 publication; originally published in 1939 as
the author's thesis, University of Illinois, 1932.
  Includes bibliographical references and index.
  ISBN 0-252-06226-4
    1. Chinese Americans—California—History.   2. California—Race
relations.   I. Daniels, Roger.   II. Title.
F870.C5S3   1991
979.4'004951—dc20   91-10876
                                                                         CIP

CONTENTS

FOREWORD

The Anti-Chinese Movement in Historical Perspective

THE ENACTMENT of the Chinese Exclusion Act ninety years ago was an important watershed in the history of American immigration legislation. It marks the beginning of a period of more than eight decades (1882-1965) in which the immigration policy of the United States was officially racist. Chinese exclusion was followed by executive agreements to restrain Japanese immigration (1907-08), the "barred zone" act of 1917, which excluded all other Asians, save Japanese and Filipinos, the National Origins Act of 1924, which not only included Japanese in the excluded group but also enacted highly discriminatory quota restrictions against Caucasian ethnic groups considered inferior. The final escalation of discrimination against Asians occurred in 1934, when, under a special provision of the Philippine Independence Act, Filipinos were restricted to a quota of fifty per year. The first significant relaxation of immigration laws against Asians took place in 1943, when Congress, in a token gesture toward a wartime ally, granted China a quota of 100. All Asian nations got similar quotas under the 1952 McCarran Walter Act. Ethnic quotas, as such, were abolished in the 1965 revision of the basic immigration statutes. Under that act fairly large numbers of Chinese have immigrated to the United States, largely from Hong Kong and Taiwan. In the year ended June 30, 1970, for example, slightly more than 14,000 Chinese entered this country as immigrants while an additional 34,000 entered as non-immigrants.[1]

Elmer Sandmeyer's 1939 book — the outgrowth of a 1932 dissertation in history at the University of Illinois — was the first modern account of an important episode in the development of organized racism in the far western United States. Prior to Sandmeyer, the anti-Chinese movement had been viewed with distaste by racist nineteenth-century historians like Hubert Howe Bancroft,[2] and had been attacked as bigoted by WASP historians like Mary Roberts Coolidge, who substituted class biases of her own. She so little understood the political dynamics of California that she could write, in 1909, of the anti-Japanese movement then coming to a head, that it was "after all a superficial demonstration confined to a class of workingmen, and reflected by political aspirants of the lower grade but ignored by the majority."[3]

[1] U.S. Immigration and Naturalization Service, *Annual Report* (Washington, 1970), p. 40.
[2] For Bancroft the best introduction is the biography by John Walton Caughey, *Hubert Howe Bancroft* (Berkeley and Los Angeles, 1946).
[3] Mary Roberts Coolidge, *Chinese Immigration* (New York, 1909), p. 253. Arno Press published a reprint in 1969.

3

Sandmeyer's approach, and it is this that sets his work off from what had gone before, was not to denigrate but to attempt to understand. In that attempt he largely succeeded. Without in any way "approving" the anti-Chinese movement, he demonstrated that its roots were in deeply felt social and economic grievances. He understood that while "diverse motives" were responsible for its growth and success, the fundamental element was racial "antagonism, reinforced by economic competition" (p. 109). His research, largely in newspapers, pamphlets, government documents, and the periodical press, established clearly and precisely the successive manifestations of anti-Chinese sentiment which coalesced into a movement that triumphed successively on the local, state, regional, and finally national level. If the writing and level of analysis are somewhat pedestrian, the work is accurate, and, in the more than three decades since its publication, no scholar has thought it necessary to redo Sandmeyer's effort. Nor is any such re-examination likely.

Only in the last decade, when, for a variety of reasons, historians were becoming more and more conscious of race and ethnicity as important factors in the American past and present, did monographic literature begin to appear that significantly supplemented, but did not replace, Sandmeyer's work. The three most important of these were, in chronological order, Gunther Barth's *Bitter Strength* (1964), Stuart C. Miller's *The Unwelcome Immigrant* (1969), and Alexander Saxton's *The Indispensable Enemy* (1971).[4]

Barth, a student of Oscar Handlin's, attempted to write a history of the Chinese in the United States in the first two decades of their experience. Seriously hampered by an almost total absence of documentary evidence telling the story from a Chinese point of view, Barth resorted heavily to the argument from analogy, comparing Chinese immigration to the United States with that of Chinese to various parts of southeast Asia. Replacing Mrs. Coolidge's Victorian sentimentality with the broad-based social science approach typical of Handlin's students, he characterized the Chinese as essentially "sojourners" but eventually becoming immigrants.

Stuart Miller like Barth eastern-trained, essayed an intellectual history of American attitudes toward the Chinese, as his subtitle shows. Despite a great deal of uncertainty — and occasionally error — about California history, Miller managed, for the first time, to integrate anti-Chinese attitudes into the mainstream of American ideas. While previous scholarship, including my own, had contended that "racism, as a pervasive doctrine, did not develop in the United States until after the Civil

[4] Gunther Barth, *Bitter Strength: A History of the Chinese in the United States, 1850-1870* (Cambridge, Mass., 1964); Stuart Creighton Miller, *The Unwelcome Immigrant: The American Image of the Chinese, 1785-1882* (Berkeley and Los Angeles, 1969); Alexander Saxton, *The Indispensable Enemy: Labor and the Anti-Chinese Movement in California* (Berkeley and Los Angeles, 1971).

War" and that no common assumptions underlay the various manifestations of national xenophobia,[5] Miller convincingly demonstrates that strong racist anti-Chinese attitudes existed in American thought long before the Chinese came. He thus added a new and perhaps crucial factor in understanding the success of the anti-Chinese movement: "the unfavorable image of the Chinese that preceded them to the United States" (p. 201).

Neither Barth nor Miller dealt directly with the anti-Chinese forces in California. This has now been done by Alexander Saxton, an established novelist before he took his doctorate at Berkeley. Writing as a historian of labor, he succeeded admirably in putting flesh and blood on some of the hitherto skeletal labor spokesmen and leaders who headed the anti-Chinese movement. Like Miller, Saxton found eastern roots for what had been assumed to be an indigenous far western movement. Where Miller examined the thoughts of men like Ralph Waldo Emerson and John Quincy Adams, Saxton discovers some of the roots of anti-Chinese sentiment in the murky ideology of Jacksonian America. His thesis, which had been sketched out years before by pioneer labor historians Ira Cross and some of his students, was that the presence of large numbers of Chinese provided the indispensable cement to hold together the relatively very strong California labor movement.

Taken conjointly, these works (and particularly Miller and Saxton) provide a needed reappraisal of Sandmeyer's perspective, if not his data. He saw the anti-Chinese movement as an essentially regional force using political leverage to gain national legislation. Pointing to the lack of a decisive national majority for either party in the late 1870s and early 1880s, he argued, quite correctly, that the Pacific states thus acquired "tremendous bargaining power" and that as a result, many national figures "championed legislative measures that they might otherwise have opposed" (p. 111). We now have been shown that on two separate intellectual levels preconditions favorable to the success of an anti-Chinese movement already existed. Above all it is necessary to see the anti-Chinese movement as a manifestation of a racism that was national, not merely regional.

ROGER DANIELS

Fredonia, N.Y.
June, 1972

---

[5] Roger Daniels, *The Politics of Prejudice: The Anti-Japanese Movement in California and the Struggle for Japanese Exclusion* (Berkeley and Los Angeles, 1962), pp. 65-68.

PREFACE

IMMIGRANTS have been the makers of America. For more than three hundred years streams of human beings have poured through our portals to fill up our borders. But the last quarter of a century has seen those streams dwindle to a mere trickle. The policy of restriction, developing through the years, was speeded up by the World War, which revealed widespread failure of the assimilative processes and convinced Americans that the influx must be stopped.

In the total volume of immigration the Chinese formed a very minor segment, but the attention which they commanded was far out of proportion to their numbers. The novelty and picturesqueness of their manner of living enlarged public interest in them and in their fate. The events incident to the restriction of their coming, the first movement against foreigners to achieve success, excited the nation's concern and pointed the way for subsequent efforts.

Numerous studies of one phase or another of the Chinese question have been made.[1] Almost without exception, however, these works have shown a distinct tendency toward a pro-Chinese bias, very largely induced by the abuse to which the immigrants were subjected, or by some special interest which the author had in them.

In making the present study the aim has been to trace the development of the movement against the Chinese in California from its beginning to the time when their exclusion was extended indefinitely. Its purpose is to show what conditions gave rise to this movement, what groups supplied the leadership, what motives actuated these groups, what obstacles they encountered, what methods were employed in attaining their ends, and the successive steps in the movement. It is obvious that, in thus limiting the scope of the investigation, many otherwise interesting matters concerning the Chinese necessarily have been omitted.

While many standard works have been used in gathering the data for this study, primarily the effort has been to discover the contemporary reaction as reflected in newspaper editorials, magazine articles, reports of conventions and investigations, laws and ordinances, treaties and public speeches. Much of this material must bear the charge of bias, or even of being false. But this does not lessen its value for this study, since we are concerned chiefly with the factors which influenced people's attitude toward the Chinese. It is now many years since one of our greatest

---

[1]Most important among these are: O. Gibson, *The Chinese in America.* Cincinnati, 1877; Ira M. Condit, *The Chinaman As We See Him,* New York, 1900; George F. Seward, *Chinese Immigration, in Its Social and Economical Aspects,* New York, 1881; Tien-lu Li, *Congressional Policy of Chinese Immigration; or, Legislation Relating to Chinese Immigration to the United States, Nashville,* 1916; Mary Roberts Coolidge, *Chinese Immigration,* New York, 1909. The last is the most comprehensive.

historical writers pointed out that men are influenced, not necessarily by what actually happens, but by what they think or understand has happened, and that frequently erroneous ideas and beliefs have had a far greater causal relation to subsequent events than the actual facts.[2]

The helpfulness of others has placed me under innumerable obligations. Professor Theodore Calvin Pease not only suggested the problem but advised me throughout the investigation. Professors Albert H. Lybyer and Avery O. Craven suggested points of view. Attendants in the libraries of the universities of Illinois, California, and Southern California, the Bancroft Library at Berkeley, the public libraries of Long Beach, Santa Monica, and Los Angeles, and the Los Angeles County Law Library have shown unforgettable courtesies and given assistance beyond compensation.

It remains only to add that all conclusions and all mistakes are my own.

E. C. S.

Santa Monica, California

---

[2]William A. Dunning, "Truth in History," *American Historical Review*, XIX, 217-229, January, 1914.

INTRODUCTION

CALIFORNIA became a part of the United States in the incidental fashion in which a farmer might catch an over-ripe apple as it fell from the tree. For decades American adventurers had been filtering into this territory, contrary to the laws of both Spain and Mexico. Mexican control was becoming more and more tenuous, and even before news of the declaration of war had reached California an American group in the north had raised the flag of revolt and independence. The work of Fremont, Sloat, and Kearny was more in the nature of authentication than of achievement.[1]

More than four years had passed after the raising of the American flag at Monterey before Congress provided for the government of this new territory. When California was finally admitted to the Union, a constitution had been formed, a full complement of state officials had been elected, and her congressmen and senators had been in Washington for months, waiting to be sworn.

Back of the impatience of the people to establish a state government was the discovery of gold. Within a year after the knowledge of this event had spread to the outside world California had changed from a slow-going province of about thirteen thousand people to a feverishly active community of almost one hundred thousand. From every continent, by every conceivable means of travel, men of every station in life crowded into California, following the lure of gold. In a remarkably short time they had spread over the hills and valleys of northern and central California. The new state government was unable to keep up with them. Consequently, the mining communities became governments unto themselves, making regulations to meet their respective needs. "When occasion demanded enforcement of the law, all joined in and the criminal soon found that the way of the transgressor was likely to lead to the end of a rope."[2]

The decade following statehood was one of restlessness and expansion, of clamor for Federal aid, and complaint because of desires unsatisfied. The population, in overwhelming proportions, was made up of men, mostly young men, adventurous, and living under social conditions in which the restraints of civilized society were lacking. Old standards of values no longer were recognized; gambling, drunkenness, and licentiousness were widely prevalent. Within a few years the best of the placers

[1] A good account of the period since the conquest is Robert Glass Cleland, *A History of California: American Period*, New York, 1922. The most complete treatment is the series edited by John Russell McCarthy and published by Powell, Los Angeles, 1929. Dealing with certain phases are: Mary Floyd Williams, *History of the San Francisco Committee of Vigilance*, Berkeley, 1921. Joseph Ellison, *California and the Nation, 1850-1869*, Berkeley, 1927. William C. Fankhauser, *A Financial History of California: Public Revenues, Debts, and Expenditures*, Berkeley, 1913. Thomas R. Bacon, "The Railroad Strike in California," *Yale Review*, III, 241-250, November, 1894. Lucille Eaves, *California Labor Legislation*, Berkeley, 1910.
[2] Owen C. Coy and Herbert C. Jones, *California's Constitution*, Los Angeles, 1930, 11.

had been worked out. Political office had become a means of plunder. Ballot box stuffing developed into a fine art. It was a time of extensive speculation and of financial irregularities. It was in the midst of conditions such as these that the Vigilance Committees of 1851 and 1856 were organized.

The great national struggle reverberated widely in California. The shibboleths of political alignment echoed national party divisions as loudly as local problems. While the number who favored slavery was small, there were many who were sympathetic with the southern wing of the Democratic party, and certain groups urged the forming of an independent government on the coast. There was some guerrilla warfare and a great deal of newspaper comment, but on the whole California was loyal to the Union and rendered notable service, both in men and in money.

The Civil War did not monopolize the attention of Californians during the second decade. An outstanding achievement was the completion, after twenty years of agitation, of the first transcontinental railroad, which opened a new era for the far west. This was the period, also, when organized labor made its first notable development. Diversified agriculture became the predominant economic interest, the mines becoming relatively less important. The development of grain farming had been handicapped by the unsettled condition of land titles, and by ignorance of what and how to plant. But a severe drouth in the winter of 1863 gave impetus to the transition from cattle raising. Many of the larger landowners were compelled to dispose of their holdings, in some cases to men who subdivided them into small farms. The fencing of farmlands tended to develop dairying and hay growing. By the end of the decade California was one of the chief wheat growing states, barley was becoming an increasingly important crop, and the raising of grapes, peaches, berries, and other fruits was becoming profitable. In addition, citrus fruits, petroleum mining, and manufacturing had made a beginning.

The decade following 1870 has been termed "The Nadir of National Disgrace." The "Whiskey Ring," the "Tweed Regime," the "Mulligan Letters," "Credit Mobilier," and other equally malodorous episodes were signs of the times. It was also the period of the first great strikes in American industry and of a very serious depression.

California had its full share of these experiences. Adjustments in the economic life of the people were still in their early stages. While the completion of the transcontinental railroad had solved the problem of transportation, it had brought many grave problems to the state: exorbitant rates, land monopoly, tax evasion, and intervention in politics. Other conditions added to the unrest and dissatisfaction: scarcity of capital and high interest rates, farm failures, inequitable taxation, corrupt and inefficient government, water monopoly, speculation, business depression, and widespread unemployment. Add to these a population of varied national elements, adventurous in spirit and without the background of a long-settled community, and it is not surprising that the period was one of many radical proposals and unwise actions. Out of this cauldron came new political parties, a new constitution, mob violence, and bitter anti-Chinese agitation.

Some of these difficulties carried over into succeeding years, but a new era of development made them seem less significant. Farmers were beginning to understand the opportunities and needs of soil and climate; large landholders, particularly the railroads, made greater efforts to place their lands upon the market and to induce settlers to come from the east; the value of the southern part of the state, especially for the growing of citrus fruits, began to be appreciated; and largely as a result of the rivalry between the Southern Pacific and Santa Fe railroads, there came the first great boom and extension of settlement in the south.

This growth did not lack for problems. The last two decades of the nineteenth century were clamorous with demands for change. Exploitation, speculation, and corruption laid heavy toll upon the state. The Southern Pacific came in for special attack because it sought to evade the taxes levied against it, denied the authority of the state to regulate rates, and was accused of dominating the politics of the state. Direct primaries, direct election of senators, the secret ballot, and woman suffrage were objects of agitation. The rapidly growing cities supplied rich fields for political bosses and grafting, climaxed by the revelations in San Francisco immediately following the great fire of 1906.

Inextricably intermingled in the varied ramifications of these developments appeared the Chinese. Welcomed at first as meeting the dire need for labor, they came in time to be looked upon as the source of most of the ills which afflicted the state. This feeling developed into a definite movement to get rid of the Chinese, or at least to prevent any increase in their numbers. During all of this period they were seldom if ever considered purely on their merits, but always from the viewpoint of their effect upon the numerous problems confronting the people of the state.

CHAPTER I

THE CHINESE COME TO CALIFORNIA

THE DATE of arrival of the first Chinese in California is not definitely known. The census of 1850 did not list the Chinese as a separate group, but figures supplied by the immigration authorities placed the total number arriving in the United States during the thirty years preceding that date at forty-six.[1] That this figure did not include recent arrivals in California is evident from the fact that there was no customs office there until after admission into the Union. Authorities generally agree that the first Chinese arrived about the time gold was discovered, and very soon they might have been seen in relatively large numbers in the mining regions. A group of the "China boys" took part in the memorial services for President Taylor and in the celebration of the admission of California into the Union.[2]

Practically all of the Chinese in California during this period came from the Kwangtung Province in southeastern China, of which Canton is the chief city. The inhabitants of this area possessed a more venturesome and independent spirit than those in the northern provinces, for throughout the Christian era they had maintained commercial relations with other parts of the world. This district had been the first to come in contact with the European traders of the sixteenth century, and for four decades of the nineteenth century Canton was the only port open to trade. From this center

. . . . adventurous emigrants have for centuries penetrated through the Indian archipelago, have pushed through the Indian Ocean to Ceylon and Arabia, have reclaimed Formosa and Hainan, have established a remarkable trade with Cochin China, Cambodia and Siam and have introduced useful arts into Java, the Philippines and the Malay Peninsula.[3]

We must distinguish at least three groups among the Chinese in California. The merchants, who ranked near the bottom in the social scale in China, were looked upon as the leaders of the Chinese in this country. These men not only handled practically all of the merchandise consumed by the Chinese population, but also dominated the "companies"

---

[1]*Statistical Review of Immigration, 1820-1910.* Report of the Immigration Commission, William P. Dillingham, Chairman. *Senate Doc. No. 756,* 61st Cong., 3d sess., 14-24.

[2]Hubert Howe Bancroft, *History of California,* San Francisco, 1888, VI, 124-130. Theodore H. Hittell, *History of California,* San Francisco, 1897, IV, 99. Condit, *The Chinaman As We See Him,* p. 15. "Memoirs of Lemuel Clarke McKeeby," *Quarterly of the California Historical Society,* III, 70, April, 1924. *Chronicle,* July 21, 1878. (San Francisco newspapers are cited without the name of the city.)

[3]Pyau Ling, "Causes of Chinese Emigration," *Annals,* XXXIX, 75. S. Wells Williams in *Report of the Joint Special Committee to Investigate Chinese Immigration, Senate Report No. 689,* 44th Cong., 2d sess., 1243-1246. (Hereafter referred to as *Report 689*). *Chinese Immigration: Its Social, Moral, and Political Effect,* Report of the Special Committee on Chinese Immigration to the California State Senate, Sacramento, 1878, 70, 83, 90, 104. E. T. Williams, *China: Yesterday and Today,* New York, 1929, 16, 17, 417-431.

to which all Chinese men belonged. These merchants enjoyed a very high reputation among American business men for integrity and business ability. There was a tendency among certain Californians to judge all Chinese by this class.[4]

The merchant group, however, constituted a very small proportion of the total Chinese population. The great majority were laborers. It was generally agreed that almost all of them were young men, with an extremely small number of homes, but industrious, frugal, sober, and quick to learn new ways; also, that they were inveterate gamblers, addicted to the use of opium, and apparently little impressed with American civilization and institutions. Most of them could read the names of the ordinary necessities of life, but very few had anything like a common school education. They went quietly about their own affairs, manifesting little inclination to intrude upon the society of other nationalities, seldom retaliating when attacked, and apparently asking only to be left alone in their pursuit of happiness.[5]

Concerning one class of Chinese in California there was little if any difference of opinion. Relatively, very few Chinese women came to America, the reasons given being that custom forbade women to leave their homes and that very few of the Chinese came expecting to remain permanently. Under these conditions the presence of great numbers of single men invited the traffic in prostitutes, which certain Chinese found to be very profitable business. For a short time after the passage of the Page Law in 1875 the traffic apparently ceased, but it was later resumed.[6]

The Chinese inherently have not been a migratory people. For many centuries they had considered their country the center of civilization, and the ties of home drew closely about them. And yet, during the nineteenth century, the Chinese in large numbers left their homes for other lands. What were the influences bringing about this migration? Political and religious freedom seem to have been unimportant. The fundamental reason is to be found in the overcrowded living conditions prevailing in parts of China, especially in the southeastern provinces. Reduction in the means of sustenance, due to drouth, flood, or plant pests, time and again has placed millions of Chinese in danger of starvation.[7]

To the overcrowded living conditions were added the devastations of war. The independent spirit of Kwangtung and Fukien provinces led them to protect the Ming dynasty against the invading Manchus in the seventeenth century. The Manchus, in retaliation, wrought havoc in

[4]*Report 689*, 489-492, 508-510, 530, 542, 711.
[5]*Report 689*, 70, 89, 407-408, 489, 756, 831, 1245, *et passim*.
[6]Gibson, *Chinese in America*, 35, 134-140. *Report 689*, 145, 405, 1247-1248. *Bulletin,* Nov. 10, 1876; Nov. 26, 29, Dec. 6, 15, 19, 1887; Jan. 10, March 6, 1888.
[7]Ta Chen, *Chinese Migrations*, Bulletin of the Bureau of Labor Statistics, No. 340; Washington, 1923, 5-7. Pyau Ling, *Annals*, XXXIX, 74-76.

these provinces. In more recent times, and coinciding with the immigration to California, a new series of wars occurred, particularly those with Great Britain and France. In each case taxes were increased to meet the costs of war and indemnity, while destruction and uncertainty brought loss and suffering to the people.[8]

Even more devastating than these foreign wars was the civil war known as the "Tai Ping Rebellion," which has been called "The greatest event in the domestic history of China during the Manchu period." Beginning at mid-century in Kwangsi province, the revolt against the weak Manchu ruler swept through the maritime provinces, occupying and plundering them for more than a decade. One writer estimated that war and disease destroyed twenty million lives, while fire and sword laid waste the most prosperous regions of China. Industry and trade were paralyzed, and unemployment led to more flourishing conditions in the contract coolie trade with Cuba, South America, and the West Indies, as well as sending thousands of immigrants to California and Australia.[9]

External influences were equally effective. In point of time the first of these was the lure of gold. The news of Marshall's discovery reached Hong Kong in the spring of 1848 and created great excitement. Shipmasters were quick to seize the opportunity, distributing placards, maps, and pamphlets concerning the "Golden Hills." The spell of the "Golden Romance" became even stronger when some of the first arrivals returned and exhibited substantial evidence of success in their venture. Nor was this attraction temporary. Throughout the period of war devastations "the call of the Golden Mountains . . . . was ringing in the air of the distressed regions of Canton." "To be starved and to be buried in the sea are the same," was the thought in the minds of thousands who fled to Hong Kong and the ships.[10]

The most constant and, on the whole, the most effective motivating force was the demand for labor. Like all frontier communities, California experienced a pronounced scarcity of labor, which was accentuated by the rush to the gold fields. The Chinese were looked upon as a veritable god-send. Women were very few, and the Chinese supplied the need for cooks, laundrymen, and the like, as well as that of the heavier work of the mines. Their importance as laborers in the earlier years is attested by the fact that the first agitation specifically concerning them was occasioned, not by their presence, but rather by an attempt to pass legislation for the enforcement in California of contracts made in China.[11]

---

[8]S. Wells Williams. *The Middle Kingdom,* New York, 1913, 2 volumes, II, 463-574, 625-689. John W. Foster, *American Diplomacy in the Orient,* Boston, 1903, 214-254.
[9]Williams, *Middle Kingdom,* II, 575-624. Payson J. Treat, *The Far East,* New York, 1928, 106-113.
[10]Coolidge, *Chinese Immigration,* 17. William Speer, *The Oldest and the Newest Empire, or China and the United States,* Hartford, 1870, 486. Pyau Ling, *Annals,* XXXIX, 80.
[11]*Senate Journal, 1852,* 67, 68, 217, 306, 307, 669-675. *Alta,* May 12, 1852. Hittell, *California,* IV, 103, 425-426.

During certain periods the greatest demand for Chinese labor came from the railroads. The Central Pacific began using them not later than the spring of 1865. Construction officials insisted that they were opposed to the use of Chinese labor, but competition with the Union Pacific and inability to procure white labor compelled them to employ the Chinese. Before the work was completed there were ten thousand of them on the pay-roll. Many of these were imported direct from China through San Francisco contracting companies. Later the Southern Pacific lines, especially in California, were built almost entirely with Chinese labor.[12] The development of other industries, such as grain farming, fruit growing, tide-land draining, and manufacturing, also employed Chinese labor. Proposals for extensive employment of Chinese in the southern states were seriously considered, and several shipments actually were made. They were used also, to a limited extent, as strike breakers in eastern factories.[13]

Transportation companies must be listed among the powerful influences promoting Chinese immigration. In the coolie trade with the West Indies and South America, ships under the American flag were very active until forbidden by the law of 1862. The transportation of Chinese to California made an equally strong appeal to American shippers. At times every available ship in Chinese waters was put into the service. In 1866 the Pacific Mail Steamship Company entered the China trade, under government subsidy, and a little later the Occidental and Oriental Steamship Company was organized as a competitor. Charles Crocker, an official of the latter company, claimed that both lines could not be run profitably without the Chinese passenger traffic. With the passenger traffic was linked the importation of Chinese goods, most of which was consumed by the Chinese themselves. It is not surprising that Californians placed the responsibility for the coming of many of the Chinese upon the steamship and railroad companies, whose lobbyists were accused of attempting to defeat restrictive legislation.[14] What has been said concerning immigration in general applies with particular force to that of the Chinese:

> While various motives and inducements have always worked together . . . . yet to one who has carefully noted all the circumstances it is scarcely an exaggeration to say that even more important than the initiative of immigrants have been the efforts of Americans and ship-owners to bring and attract them. . . . . The desire to get cheap labor, to take in passenger fares, and to sell land have probably brought more immigrants than the hard conditions of Europe, Asia, and Africa have sent.[15]

---

[12]*Report 689*, 599-600, 667, 674, 723 ff. *Memoirs of Cornelius Cole*, New York, 1908, 182-184. Charles Crocker to Cole.

[13]*Alta*, July 13, 15, 27, 29, 1869; Jan. 7, 9, May 23, July 28, 1870. *Bulletin*, July 8, 28, 1870. St. Louis *Democrat*, July 12, 1870. *Report 689*, 550. *Senate Exec. Doc. No. 116*, 41st Cong., 2d sess.

[14]*Bulletin*, Dec. 10, 1877, Feb. 18, Oct. 9, 1879, May 9, 1893. *Chronicle*, Feb. 3, 4, 6, 15, 16, 28, April 9, 10, 1902. For the earlier activities see *Report 689*, 673; *House Exec. Doc. No. 105*, 34th Cong., 1st sess., 67-75, 148-151; *Senate Exec. Doc. No. 30*, 36th Cong., 1st sess:, 185, 424.

[15]John R. Commons, *Races and Immigrants in America*, New York, 1920, 107-108. The question of contract immigration is discussed in a later chapter.

Statements regarding the number of Chinese in California during the early years are very greatly in conflict. They were not listed in the census of 1850, but in 1852 the Chinese Companies estimated that there were twenty-five thousand in the state. Two years later so many desired to leave China that brokers found difficulty in providing transportation. Californians have been accused of grossly exaggerating the volume of this immigration, but in view of the difficulty in procuring accurate figures this exaggeration is not surprising. Table I gives what are perhaps the best available statistics on Chinese immigration to America.[16]

In comparing these statistics one is impressed by discrepancies between the various sources. But these discrepancies are more apparent

TABLE I.—CHINESE ARRIVALS IN THE UNITED STATES, 1852-1884*

Year	Immigration Commission	Bureau of Immigration	San Francisco Customs House
1852	0	0	20,026
1853	42	42	4,270
1854	13,100	13,100	16,084
1855	3,526	3,526	3,329
1856	4,733	4,733	4,807
1857	5,944	x2,580	5,924
1858	5,128	7,183	5,427
1859	3,457	3,215	3,175
1860	5,467	6,117	7,341
1861	7,518	6,094	8,430
1862	3,633	4,174	8,175
1863	7,214	5,280	6,432
1864	2,975	5,240	2,682
1865	2,942	3,702	3,095
1866	2,385	1,872	2,242
1867	3,863	3,519	4,290
1868	x5,157	6,707	11,081
1869	12,874	12,874	14,990
1870	15,740	15,740	10,870
1871	7,135	7,135	5,540
1872	7,788	7,788	9,770
1873	20,292	20,291	17,075
1874	13,776	13,776	16,085
1875	16,437	16,437	18,021
1876	22,781	22,781	y15,481
1877	10,594	10,594	9,468
1878	8,992	8,992	6,675
1879	9,604	9,604	6,969
1880	5,802	5,802	5,950
1881	11,890	11,890	18,561
1882	39,579	39,579	z26,902
1883	8,031	8,031	.....
1884	279	4,009	.....

*Sources for these figures, respectively: *Statistical Review*, 24-35; Jenks, Lauck, and Smith, *The Immigration Problem*, 692, Chart II; Cal. Senate, *Chinese Immigration*, 236. x, Change from calendar to fiscal year. y, Figures following are from the *Alta*, March 3, 1882, and the *Bulletin*, Aug. 10, 1882. z, Jan. 1 to Aug. 4 only. It should be noted that the first two columns apply to all United States ports, while the third refers only to one.

[16]For statements on early immigration see Hittell, *California*, IV, 98-99; Bancroft, *California*, VI, 124-130; *House Exec. Doc. No. 105*, 34th Cong., 1st sess.; *Assembly Journal, 1853*, Appendix, Doc. 28; Gibson, *Chinese in America*, 20; *Alta*, May 12, 1852, March 3, April 20, May 10, 1854.

than real. With a very few exceptions they are due either to a difference in the area covered or to the fact that some are for the calendar year while others are for the fiscal year. It may be noted that during the fiscal years 1873-1876 there occurred the largest continuous influx of the preceding twenty-five years, lending a background for the intensified feeling against the Chinese manifested during these years.

Of greater significance, perhaps, was the number of Chinese actually present at any one time. Every year hundreds returned to China, and during some years, prior to 1868, more departed than arrived. Californians were accused of exaggerating the number actually in the state, but this is not surprising, since the Chinese were a very mobile element in the population, owing to the seasonal character of many of their occupations. Perhaps the most reliable basis of estimate was the membership of the Chinese Companies. These organizations covered the entire coast, and reported 58,300 in 1866 and 148,600 in 1876. It may be worthwhile to compare these figures with those of the United States census:

TABLE 2.—CHINESE POPULATION*

	1860	1870	1880
Chinese in the United States.............	......	63,199	105,465
Chinese in California....................	34,933	49,277	75,132
Chinese in San Francisco................	2,719	12,022	21,745

*Tenth Census of the United States, I, 382, 399, with Cal. Senate, Chinese Immigration, 109, and Gibson, Chinese in America, 21. See also Alta, July 7, 1866, April 13, 1876, and Report 689, 12, 156.

The number of women among the Chinese immigrants to California was small. Just how small their numbers were in proportion to the total may be seen from the following comparison of Chinese and European immigration:

TABLE 3.—IMMIGRATION, BY SEX, 1820-1910*

Period	European		Chinese		San Francisco
	Per cent		Per cent		Population
	Males	Females	Males	Females	Per cent Males
1820-67.............	59.7	40.3	No data	No data	1850....	93
1870...............	60.9	39.1	92.9	7.1	1860....	79
1871-80............	61.3	38.7	90.2	9.8	1870....	76
1881-90............	61.1	38.9	99.0	1.0	1880....	71
1891-00............	62.3	37.7	96.9	3.1	1890....	68
1901-10............	69.8	30.2	94.4	5.6	1900....	65

*Statistical Review, Vol. 7, pp. 30-44. Eaves, California Labor Legislation, 3. The San Francisco statistics are based upon figures procured by Dr. Eaves from Dr. Coolidge.

An analysis of these data indicates an almost constantly increasing disproportion in the percentage of males among the immigrants from Europe, with a very noticeable flare in that direction during the last decade when they were coming in unprecedented numbers. Meanwhile, San Francisco manifested a constant trend in the direction of an equilibrium between the sexes. Among the Chinese, however, a broken tendency is apparent. During the decade of the 'seventies, when the volume of immigration was greatest, the proportion of women shows a notable increase. During the decade of the first Exclusion Law, however, they almost ceased coming, while during the two decades following they show increasing proportions.

California was a frontier state in every sense of the word. All parts of the state did not develop at the same time nor at the same rate. Hence the distribution of the population of the state showed a tendency to vary from decade to decade. This tendency was accentuated by the change from an economy based very largely upon mining during the first decade to one predominantly agricultural in the second, and then to one of increasing industrialization and urbanization in subsequent years.

A similar variation in the distribution of the Chinese is to be noted, although the trend does not always follow that of the total population. In the early years the great majority of the Chinese went to the mining regions, because these places offered the largest reward. But after 1860 agriculture, domestic service, railway construction, and manufacturing were taking them to other parts of the state. The numbers of Chinese and of whites in the different counties for three decades are given in Table 4.

This table indicates that, while California as a whole was steadily increasing in population, this increase was by no means regular over the state. Some of the counties show decreases for one decade and increases for the next. Without exception these counties were mining centers, and the fluctuation in population indicates the changing fortunes of the mining industry. It may be noted that the Chinese population of these counties fluctuated also. Sometimes this followed fairly closely that of the whites; at other times an increase in the number of Chinese accompanied a decrease in the white population. This was probably due to the Chinese taking over the less productive fields when these were deserted by the whites.

Table 5 shows the proportion of Chinese to whites in California. The figures indicate the changing conditions relative to the employment of Chinese in different parts of the state. Between 1860 and 1870 only nine counties showed a lower proportion of Chinese, while in twenty-seven counties the proportion was greater. In 1880 the proportion of Chinese showed an increase over 1870 in thirty-five counties, and fourteen

TABLE 4.—WHITES AND CHINESE IN CALIFORNIA: BY COUNTIES*

Counties	1860		1870		1880	
	Whites	Chinese	Whites	Chinese	Whites	Chinese
Alameda............	8,548	193	22,106	1,939	57,785	4,386
Alpine..............	.....	.....	676	8	521	17
Amador............	8,252	2,568	7,883	1,627	9,924	1,115
Butte..............	9,737	2,177	9,197	2,082	14,270	3,793
Calaveras..........	12,546	3,657	7,405	1,441	7,832	1,037
Colusa.............	2,165	9	5,389	271	11,698	970
Contra Costa.......	5,185	2	8,271	160	11,712	732
Del Norte..........	1,341	338	1,009	217	1,731	434
El Dorado..........	15,515	4,762	8,589	1,560	8,869	1,484
Fresno.............	999	309	3,259	427	7,891	753
Humboldt..........	2,498	37	6,025	39	13,313	241
Inyo...............	.....	.....	1,608	29	2,197	90
Kern...............	.....	.....	2,193	143	4,563	702
Klamath...........	1,220	533	1,081	542	.....	.....
Lake...............	.....	.....	2,825	119	5,339	469
Lassen.............	.....	.....	1,309	17	2,958	50
Los Angeles........	9,221	11	14,720	234	31,707	1,169
Marin..............	3,097	4	6,394	361	9,791	1,327
Mariposa...........	4,303	1,843	3,364	1,084	3,395	697
Mendocino.........	2,905	5	6,865	129	11,185	346
Merced............	1,114	0	2,548	186	5,015	575
Modoc.............	.....	.....	.....	.....	3,955	17
Mono..............	.....	.....	386	42	7,082	363
Monterey..........	4,305	6	9,429	230	10,648	372
Napa..............	5,448	17	6,725	263	12,160	905
Nevada............	14,138	2,147	16,334	2,627	17,567	3,003
Placer.............	10,819	2,392	8,850	2,410	11,882	2,190
Plumas............	3,851	399	3,571	911	4,761	871
Sacramento.........	21,692	1,731	22,725	3,595	28,923	4,892
San Benito.........	.....	.....	.....	.....	5,255	242
San Bernardino.....	2,504	0	3,964	16	6,988	123
San Diego..........	1,249	0	4,838	70	6,674	229
San Francisco.......	52,866	2,719	136,059	12,022	210,496	21,745
San Joaquin........	9,106	139	19,193	1,629	21,990	1,997
San Luis Obispo.....	1,621	0	4,567	59	8,783	183
San Mateo.........	3,088	6	6,098	519	8,031	596
Santa Barbara......	3,178	0	7,484	109	9,135	227
Santa Clara........	11,646	22	24,536	1,525	32,110	2,695
Santa Cruz.........	4,688	6	8,532	156	12,085	523
Shasta.............	3,895	415	3,529	574	7,066	1,334
Sierra.............	9,122	2,208	4,781	810	5,337	1,252
Siskiyou...........	6,992	515	5,329	1,441	6,461	1,568
Solano.............	7,092	14	15,870	920	17,387	993
Sonoma............	11,587	51	19,184	473	24,623	904
Stanislaus..........	2,002	192	6,189	306	8,186	518
Sutter.............	3,348	2	4,791	208	4,845	266
Tehama............	3,242	104	3,166	294	8,218	774
Trinity............	3,370	1,638	1,951	1,099	2,780	1,951
Tulare.............	3,262	13	4,391	99	10,757	324
Tuolumne..........	14,095	1,962	6,556	1,524	6,612	805
Ventura............	.....	.....	.....	.....	4,849	129
Yolo..............	4,683	6	9,318	395	11,015	608
Yuba..............	11,582	1,781	8,362	2,337	8,824	2,146

*Tenth Census of the United States, I, 382. Blank spaces indicate that the county named had not yet been created, except in the case of Klamath, which in 1874 was changed to Modoc. Owen C. Coy, The Genesis of California Counties, Berkeley, 1923, 24-38.

TABLE 5.—NUMBER OF CHINESE TO 1000 WHITES IN CALIFORNIA: BY COUNTIES*

County	1860	1870	1880	County	1860	1870	1880
Alameda..........	23	88	76	Plumas..........	104	256	185
Alpine............	...	12	33	Sacramento.......	80	159	169
Amador...........	312	208	112	San Benito.......	...	...	46
Butte.............	222	227	270	San Bernardino...	...	4	18
Calaveras.........	294	196	132	San Diego........	...	14	34
Colusa...........	4	50	83	San Francisco.....	52	88	104
Contra Costa......	1	19	62	San Joaquin......	15	86	91
Del Norte.........	250	215	256	San Luis Obispo...	...	13	21
El Dorado.........	312	181	169	San Mateo.......	2	86	75
Fresno............	312	132	95	Santa Barbara....	...	15	25
Humboldt.........	15	6	18	Santa Clara......	2	62	84
Inyo..............	...	18	41	Santa Cruz.......	1	18	43
Kern.............	...	65	159	Shasta...........	11	164	189
Klamath..........	454	500	...	Sierra...........	244	169	238
Lake.............	...	42	88	Siskiyou.........	74	270	244
Lassen............	...	13	17	Solano...........	2	58	51
Los Angeles.......	1	16	37	Sonoma..........	4	25	37
Marin............	1	56	137	Stanislaus........	96	50	63
Mariposa..........	435	323	208	Sutter...........	6	43	55
Mendocino........	2	19	31	Tehama..........	32	93	94
Merced...........	...	73	115	Trinity..........	500	588	714
Modoc............	...	...	4	Tulare..........	4	23	30
Mono.............	...	109	51	Tuolumne........	141	233	122
Monterey.........	...	244	35	Ventura.........	...	...	27
Napa.............	3	39	75	Yolo.............	1	43	55
Nevada...........	152	161	172	Yuba............	154	286	244
Placer............	222	278	185				

*Based upon the *Tenth Census of the United States*, I, 382.

counties had a decrease. Particularly in the mining counties the increasing proportion was due, not so much to a larger number of Chinese, as to a decrease in the number of whites.

As part of the background for the later national interest in the question of exclusion the distribution of the Chinese among the states becomes significant. For this purpose it is necessary to compare only the figures of 1870 and 1880 (Table 6). These figures indicate that in 1870 their numbers east of the Rockies were very small, many states and territories having not a single Chinese in their population. In 1880, however, only North Carolina and Vermont reported no Chinese. And while the numbers in some of the states were very small, the fact that there were any at all was accepted as proof that they might be expected to distribute themselves over the entire country in the event of continued immigration.

Several of the major occupations in which the Chinese were employed have been mentioned. As the years passed their employment became more diversified, so that it would be impossible to enumerate all of the occupations in which they were engaged. As early as 1869 one writer gave the following list of the economic activities of the Chinese in Cali-

TABLE 6.—CHINESE IN THE UNITED STATES, BY STATES AND TERRITORIES*

State	1870	1880	State	1870	1880
Alabama...........	0	4	Missouri..........	3	91
Arizona............	20	1,630	Montana..........	1,949	1,765
Arkansas..........	98	133	Nebraska..........	0	18
California.........	49,277	75,132	Nevada...........	3,152	5,416
Colorado..........	7	612	New Hampshire....	0	14
Connecticut........	2	123	New Jersey........	5	170
Dakota............	0	238	New Mexico.......	0	57
Delaware..........	0	1	New York.........	29	909
Florida............	0	18	North Carolina.....	0	0
Georgia............	1	17	Ohio..............	1	109
Idaho..............	4,274	3,379	Oregon............	3,330	9,510
Illinois............	1	209	Pennsylvania......	13	148
Indiana............	0	29	Rhode Island......	0	27
Iowa..............	3	33	South Carolina.....	1	9
Kansas............	0	19	Tennessee.........	0	25
Kentucky..........	1	10	Texas.............	25	136
Louisiana..........	71	489	Utah..............	445	501
Maine.............	1	8	Vermont...........	0	0
Maryland..........	2	5	Virginia...........	4	6
Massachusetts......	87	229	Washington........	234	3,186
Michigan..........	1	27	West Virginia......	0	5
Minnesota.........	0	24	Wisconsin.........	0	16
Mississippi........	16	51	Wyoming..........	143	914

*Based upon the *Tenth Census of the United States*, I, 379. Idaho, Montana, North Carolina, and Vermont are the only states which did not show an increase, the first two, perhaps, because of a decline n mining activity. The Dakotas are combined and Oklahoma is omitted.

fornia: woolen factories, knitting mills, railroad building, highway and wharf construction, borax beds, farms, dairies, hop plantations, small fruit farms, kitchens, wood cutting, land clearing, potato digging, salt works, liquor manufacturing, cigar and cigarette making, the manufacture of slippers, pantaloons, vests, shirts, drawers, overalls, and shoes, tin shops, shoe blacking, fishing, gardening, poultry and pig raising, peddling, cabinet making, carving, whip and harness making, brickmaking, washermen, house servants, coal heavers, deck hands, cabin servants, sailors, mining, vineyard laborers, and laborers in the tule lands. In 1877 one newspaper estimated that there were approximately eighteen thousand Chinese employed in San Francisco factories, and declared that any sudden expulsion would throw business into confusion.[17]

The wages received by the Chinese varied with the time, place, and occupation. The list in Table 7 is probably as accurate as any. This report estimated that the living costs of a Chinese laborer were from eight to ten dollars a month, that seventy-five per cent of his food and eighty per cent of his clothing were imported, and that more than half of his yearly wage was sent out of the country.

[17]*Alta*, Dec. 27, 28, 1877. For the list of occupations see the *Overland Monthly*, II, 231-239, March, 1869.

TABLE 7.—WAGES OF CHINESE LABORERS IN CALIFORNIA, 1883-1884*

Occupation	Rate	With Board?
Domestics................................	$18-25 monthly	Yes
Cooks.....................................	10-30 monthly	Yes
Cultivators of soil........................	25-30 monthly	Yes
Laundrymen..............................	6-12 monthly	Yes
Farm laborers............................	20-25 monthly	Yes
Brick makers.............................	25-35 monthly	No
Slipper makers...........................	4-5 weekly	No
Bag makers..............................	4.50-6 weekly	No
Miners...................................	1.50-2 daily	Yes
In canneries..............................	.75-1.25 daily	No
Boot and shoe makers.....................	.75-1.75 daily	No
Cigar makers.............................	4-12 per 1000	No

*First Biennial Report of the State Bureau of Labor Statistics of California, 1883-1884, Sacramento, 1884, 166-167.

An ever-increasing number of the Chinese were engaged in trade or other independent business. In 1879 the city license office of San Francisco reported that a total of 1,327 licenses had been issued to Chinese tradesmen. A similar development was reported in such cities as Sacramento, San Jose, Stockton, and Marysville.[18] The more important of these tradesmen in San Francisco maintained their own "Merchants' Exchange." Indeed, Chinese merchants became so aggressive that many Californians claimed they would monopolize many of the industries in which they were engaged. They were reported as dominating the boot and shoe industry, broom manufacturing, cigar making, and Chinese marine insurance and foreign exchange. A movement of unusual importance was suspected when a report came that a Chinese steamship company was planning to run liners from Chinese ports to Honolulu and San Francisco. The arrival of the "Ho Chung" seemed to confirm these suspicions.[19]

The conditions under which the Chinese lived in California seem to have been determined very largely by three factors: first, by the fact that the overwhelming majority were males and single; second, by the segregating effect of racial prejudice and antagonism; and third, by the customs and usages brought by the immigrants from their native environment. The last, which was largely responsible for the other two, deserves further consideration.

China is a nation with one of the longest continuous identities of any people in existence. But like a great river system it has been subject to repeated lateral infusions. These two factors—age and repeated in-

[18]Post, Oct. 5, 1878, Alta, Sept. 1, 1879, Call, Aug. 31, 1879, Chronicle, Sept. 2, 1879.
[19]Condit, op. cit., 16-17. Post, July 25, 1878, Oct. 24, 1879. Chronicle, Feb. 7, 1879, Sept. 14, 1880. Call, July 24, 1878, Oct. 29, 30, 31, Nov. 2, 1879. Report 689, 313. "If the Ho Chung were the first vessel of a new trade her arrival might be hailed with satisfaction. But . . . . she is only a stage in the advancing Mongolization of an American state." Bulletin, Aug. 12, 1880.

vasions and assimilations—undoubtedly have had great influence in shaping the character of the Chinese people, particularly their conservatism, fatalism, and ability to adapt themselves to changing conditions. Under the Empire the government was patriarchal. This characteristic was evident, not only in the relationship to the central government, but also in the almost universal prevalence of ancestor worship, in the absolute power of the head of the family over its members, and in the fact that the family and not the individual was the social unit.

Under these conditions laws were created by edict, not by legislation. But more important for social control was the inculcation of filial piety and of loyalty to one's family and clan, which made orderly conduct a matter of family pride. To this should be added the fact that the officials were organized into a hierarchy of such character that each rank exercised a strict surveillance over the one next below, and also that families and clans were held responsible for the wrong-doing of their members. Everyone was so intimately involved in the meshes of the social organization that the individual, instead of setting himself against the power of society, endured minor wrongs and exactions. Officials made of grafting a fine art, and since each hoped at some time to profit from the system, no one informed on anyone else. The Emperor's edict, however, passed through so many hands that its force was greatly weakened by the time it reached the subjects for whom it was intended. On the other hand, officials seeking confessions from those accused of crime made such extensive use of torture that more died of this than were legally executed. Because of these conditions the average Chinese kept away from the officials and settled his problems in his own fashion, either by force or by compromise.[20]

One other form of group organization, besides the family and the clan, was the guild. In China these were of four types: craft, merchant, community, and provincial. It was the last of these which attracted the greatest attention in California. The Chinese were closely attached to their home districts, and even inter-provincial migrations were not common. When they did go to other parts of the Empire they tended to unite with others from their province and form a provincial guild. In California there were six of these, with headquarters in San Francisco, and known as the "Chinese Six Companies." Since practically all of the Chinese in California came from five departments of the Kwangtung Province, there was one company for each of these departments, and one for those from other districts. Control was in the hands of the merchant members, and a membership fee of ten dollars was charged all who joined, which included practically all of the Chinese on the coast.

---

[20] S. Wells Williams, *Middle Kingdom*, I, 380-384, 472-482, 507-516; II, 135-187. E. 'T. Williams, *China*, 51-66.

The houses maintained by the companies served as hotels and restaurants for newcomers and for those temporarily in the city or who were ill. The companies undertook to settle any disputes arising among their members, or to help those who became involved in the courts; to care for the sick, bury the dead, and either care for their tombs or return their bones to their native land; also, to prevent any member who had not settled all debts from returning to China. They denied, however, having anything to do with the coolie traffic or with the importation of Chinese prostitutes.[21]

From the very beginning the Chinese immigrants tended to isolate themselves from other nationalities, and every community into which they came soon had its Chinese quarter. Homes were rare and the tendency to overcrowding notorious. Old landmarks, such as hotels and churches, were taken over by the Chinese and converted into crowded tenements. This segregation was not altogether involuntary. It was the only region where the Chinese could have a social life of their own, with such important institutions as the Six Companies, temples, theatres, newspapers, and tongs. But "Chinatown" supplied the basis for early and frequent criticism and for innumerable investigations. The fury of the attack was not lessened by the fact that, since the district was neither cleaned nor policed by the regular force, but by a special group paid by the Chinese, the city was at least partly responsible for the conditions existing there.[22]

The position of the Chinese in California has been admirably summarized by one of the State's leading historians:

Once in California, the Chinese kept almost entirely to themselves, did not understand the white man, had no desire to associate with him, and refused to adopt his customs or manner of life. The Californian, on the other hand, saw in the Chinaman only an inferior being, simple in some ways but cannier than a Scot in others, who lived in squalor and stench, spoke an outlandish jargon, worked with a patience and industry beyond comprehension, worshipped strange gods, suffered from strange diseases, practised strange vices, ate strange foods, regarded China as the land of the blessed, thrived under standards of living no white man could endure, administered his own law in his own way through his own agents, without much regard for the officials and statutes of the Sovereign State of California, suffered with helpless stoicism whatever indignities were thrust upon him (partly because he had no vote), and represented but the far flung skirmish line of an army of 400,000,000 beings like unto himself. No wonder California became alarmed![23]

---

[21]Lai Chuen Chen, *Remarks of the Chinese Merchants of San Francisco upon Governor Bigler's Message*, San Francisco, 1855, 6-14. S. Wells Williams, *Chinese Immigration*, New York, 1879, 11. *Middle Kingdom*, I, 482-487. E. T. Williams, *China*, 188-204. Persia Crawford Campbell, *Chinese Coolie Emigration to countries within the British Empire*, London, 1923, 30. *Overland Monthly*, I, 221-227, September, 1868. Cal. Senate, *Chinese Immigration*, 91, 109-110, 137.

[22]*Report 689*, 126-133, 159-169, 210-219, 229-231. Ching Chao Wu, "Chinatowns: A Study of Symbiosis and Assimilation," University of Chicago, *Abstracts of Theses* (Humanities Series. VII, 351-354). Chicago, 1930.

[23]Cleland, *California*, 416.

Chapter II

THE BASES OF ANTI-CHINESE SENTIMENT

No SINGLE CAUSE furnished the motivation of the anti-Chinese movement in California. It was only through the combination of a variety of motives, appealing to diversified groups, together with an auspicious political situation, that the movement for the exclusion of the Chinese was able to succeed.

The range of the motives which served as the bases of the anti-Chinese sentiment in California may be seen in two statements made in 1876. According to the first of these, Californians were convinced,

That he is a slave, reduced to the lowest terms of beggarly economy, and is no fit competitor for an American freeman.

That he herds in scores, in small dens, where a white man and wife could hardly breathe, and has none of the wants of a civilized white man.

That he has neither wife nor child, nor expects to have any.

That his sister is a prostitute from instinct, religion, education, and interest, and degrading to all around her.

That American men, women and children cannot be what free people should be, and compete with such degraded creatures in the labor market.

That wherever they are numerous, as in San Francisco, by a secret machinery of their own, they defy the law, keep up the manners and customs of China, and utterly disregard all the laws of health, decency and morality.

That they are driving the white population from the state, reducing laboring men to despair, laboring women to prostitution, and boys and girls to hoodlums and convicts.

That the health, wealth, prosperity and happiness of our State demand their expulsion from our shores.[1]

The official spokesman of San Francisco before the Joint Special Committee of Congress expressed a similar view:

The burden of our accusation against them is that they come in conflict with our labor interests; that they can never assimilate with us; that they are a perpetual, unchanging, and unchangeable alien element that can never become homogeneous; that their civilization is demoralizing and degrading to our people; that they degrade and dishonor labor; that they can never become citizens, and that an alien, degraded labor class, without desire of citizenship, without education, and without interest in the country it inhabits, is an element both demoralizing and dangerous to the community within which it exists.

These charges were repeated in so many speeches, editorials, and other forms of expression that one can hardly escape the conviction that they represented widely prevalent belief.[2]

The contents of these charges may be considered under three heads: the economic, the moral and religious, and the social and political. Of the charges which may be designated as economic none was more

---

[1]*Marin Journal,* Mar. 30, 1876.
[2]Quotation is from *Report 689,* 31. See also *ibid.,* 1001-1003. *Cong. Record,* 44th Cong., 1st sess., 2850-2857. *Argonaut,* Oct. 27, Nov. 3, 10, 17, Dec. 1, 29, 1877.

frequently nor more persistently used than that of coolieism. While the evidence thus far presented indicates that the motivating influences of Chinese immigration were essentially like those operating among Europeans, Californians were convinced that Chinese laborers came to this country under servile or "coolie" contracts. Senator Sargent had the support of widespread public opinion when he insisted that, in spite of laws forbidding the importation of coolies, the Chinese coming to California were not free, but were bound to service for a term of years, the faithful performance of their contracts being secured by their families at home, and that while these contracts were void under our laws, they were made effective by the superstitions of the coolies.[3]

These charges were not new to Californians. The attempt to pass the Tingley Bill in 1852 for the enforcement of contracts made in China had been defeated only after bitter debate. The following year members of the Chinese Companies admitted that they had imported men under contract but, finding it unprofitable, had discontinued the practice. Californians were inclined to accept this evidence, and the statements of Frederick F. Low to the effect that Chinese laborers were too poor to finance their passage, and of Thomas H. King that practically all Chinese men came under contract for a definite period of years, rather than the report of a special committee of the legislature in 1862 or the later statement of the attorney of the Six Companies denying the existence of coolie contracts among the Chinese in California.[4] Public opinion, as represented in the press, tended to identify Chinese labor with Negro slavery in the south, a slavery not of law, but of condition and custom.

> Coolies are such pauper Chinese as are hired in bulk and by conract at Chinese ports, to be hired out by the contracting party in this or any other foreign country to which by the terms of the contract they are to be shipped. The contracting parties for California are the Six Companies, and they have imported more than nine-tenths of all the Chinese who have come to this state . . . . When the coolie arrives here he is as rigidly under the control of the contractor who brought him as ever an African slave was under his master in South Carolina or Louisiana. There is no escape from the contractor or the contract.[5]

This conviction of Californians was buttressed by the knowledge that traffic in Chinese "coolie" or contract labor was being carried on to the West Indies and South America. The term "coolie" had been applied to the Chinese by foreigners, and in the sense in which it generally was used it meant simply common laborers, with no implication whatever of involuntary servitude. But the term came to be applied to the system of

---

[3]*Cong. Record*, 44th Cong., 1st sess., 2850-2854. The distinction which Sargent made between legal and customary control was probably more important than his contemporaries realized. See Roy M. Lockenour, "The Chinese Court System," *Temple Law Quarterly*, Jan., 1931, 253-259.
[4]*Report 689*, 44, 82, 93. *Senate Journal*, 1852, 67-68, 192, 217, 669-675. *Assembly Journal*, 1853, 233; Appendix, Doc. 28. *Legislative Journals*, 1862, III, Appendix No. 23.
[5]*Chronicle*, Mar. 6, 1879. See also *Bulletin*, April 1, 1876, Feb. 10, 1879. *Call*, Oct. 24, 1880. Sacramento *Bee*, May 23, 1876.

transporting contract laborers to the mines and plantations of the Spanish and British, and was soon current in connection with the Chinese in California. The "coolie traffic" to the West Indies and South America had begun before the middle of the century, and by 1871 more than one hundred thousand had been sent to Cuba alone.[6]

Most of this traffic centered at Macao, Amoy, and Hong Kong. The recruiting, which was handled either by "coolie brokers" on a commission basis or by merchants as a speculative proposition, was permeated with fraud and graft, kidnapping, and inveigling into gambling debts. The Chinese spoke of the traffic as "the buying and selling of pigs." Conditions in transit can be compared only with the horrors of the "middle passage" of the African slave trade. Little provision was made for the comfort of the coolies, and instances were not infrequent of revolts among them, resulting often in death and destruction. The risks involved in the traffic made it difficult to procure ships.[7]

The reprehensible methods of many of those engaged in the traffic furnished many perplexing problems for the consuls in China. The Chinese government was opposed to the traffic, but did little about it, largely because of the lack of consuls in foreign countries. In 1862 Americans were prohibited from participating in it. Within the British Empire the government had exercised a certain amount of supervision over the trade from the beginning, and by 1874 had assumed full control so far as its own subjects and territories were concerned. The worst elements came to center at Macao, and the supervision of the Portuguese government was very lax. Finally, through the efforts of the British and Chinese governments and by action of Portugal, the Macao traffic was terminated, leaving only Hong Kong and the treaty ports. The Chinese government, however, barred the traffic from the treaty ports after the report of an investigating committee sent to Cuba in 1876. There is evidence, however, that the trade continued illegally for some years longer.[8]

What connection, if any, existed between this traffic and the immigration of Chinese to California? As we have seen, American ships had been rather extensively engaged in the traffic. Reports of consular officials, admissions by members of the Chinese Companies, and the attempt to pass the Tingley "Coolie Bill" are evidence that in the early

---

[6] *House Exec. Doc. No. 1,* 42d Cong., 2d sess., 221-222. Campbell, *Chinese Coolie Emigration,* 86-160, is the best discussion of this traffic. See also *Senate Exec. Doc. No. 30,* 36th Cong., 1st sess., 64. *House Exec. Doc. No. 105,* 34th Cong., 1st sess., 152-154.

[7] Campbell, *op. cit.,* 95-105. *House Exec. Doc. No. 1,* 42d Cong., 2d sess., 194-210. *House Report No. 443,* 36th Cong., 1st sess. *Senate Exec. Doc. No. 22,* 35th Cong., 2d sess., 623. *Alta,* Oct. 4, 1870.

[8] *Call* and *Post,* April 10, 1878. Campbell, *op. cit.,* 114, 120, 135-158. Miss Campbell says of the committee which went to Cuba, "The Commission's Report is perhaps the most serious indictment ever made by responsible officials against a labor system." *Senate Exec. Doc. No. 116,* 41st Cong., 2d sess., 3. *House Exec. Doc. No. 1,* 42d Cong., 2d sess., 194-207. *House Exec. Doc. No. 1,* 43d Cong., 1st sess., 203.

years Chinese came to California under such contracts. Californians were convinced that the traffic was being continued long after it had been prohibited. As proof they pointed to the apparent control exercised by the Chinese Six Companies over the immigrants, to the fact that Chinese laborers were brought into the country in large numbers for the railroads and other corporations, and to the plausible statements of men who were presumed to know the facts.[9] On the other hand, the Chinese Six Companies earnestly denied that they controlled these laborers, and the men who knew them best insisted that they were not imported under the notorious coolie system. The difference, however, seems to have been chiefly one of degree rather than of kind. The evidence is conclusive that by far the majority of the Chinese who came to California had their transportation provided by others and bound themselves to make repayment. In the words of one of the most thorough students of this problem,

> There is no doubt that the greater part of the Chinese emigration to California was financed and controlled by merchant brokers, acting either independently or through Trading Guilds. . . . . Under the credit-ticket system Chinese brokers paid the expenses of the coolie emigration. Until the debt so incurred by the coolie was paid off the broker had a lien on his services—a lien that might or might not be sold to a bona fide employer of labor. . . . . By the credit-ticket system . . . . was made possible the large emigration of Southern Chinese to U. S. A., Canada and Australia which commenced during the fifties of last century and continued until it was gradually restricted or prohibited by the legislatures of these English-speaking states.[10]

Foreigners in China differed in their statements regarding this traffic. Peter Parker, S. Wells Williams, and Sir Arthur Edward Kennedy, colonial governor at Hong Kong, declared that the shipments to California were not of the notorious contract coolie order, and that they were so recognized by the Chinese. United States Consuls Denny and Bailey, however, insisted that there was no difference between those going to California and those bound for Cuba and other places in the West Indies and South America. The most evident difference was that, while the contracts of the "coolie traffic" were sold and the coolie had nothing to say as to whom he should serve, the broker retained the "credit ticket" of the California immigrant. In other words, the laborer's obligation was direct to the broker, and while the latter exercised a close supervision over him, the laborer was free to choose his employer so long as he made his monthly payments.[11]

Californians, in constantly increasing numbers, either doubted that this difference existed or discounted its significance, holding that the living

---

[9]*Report 689*, 76, 82-83, 93, 406, 674. James D. Richardson (Comp.), *Messages and Papers of the Presidents, 1789-1897*, 10 volumes, Washington, 1900, VII, 288.
[10]Campbell, *Chinese Coolie Emigration*, XVII, 78.
[11]Campbell, *op. cit.*, 29. *Report 689*, 83, 1245-1246. *Cong. Globe*, 37th Cong., 2d sess., 351. House *Exec. Doc. No. 105*, 34th Cong., 1st sess., 75. *House Exec. Doc. No. 1*, 43d Cong., 2d sess., 567. *Consular Reports, 1880-1881*, 175-180. *House Exec. Doc. No. 60*, 46th Cong., 2d sess. *Chronicle*, March 6, 1880. *Bulletin*, Nov. 27, 1880.

and working conditions of the Chinese were those of slavery, even if legal evidence were lacking. The absence of tangible evidence was accounted for on the ground that the agreements were never brought into American courts but were enforced by Chinese methods. Substantial proof of this was found in the control exercised by the Companies through an agreement with the shipping concerns, that no ticket should be sold to a Chinese unless he presented a certificate from his Company to the effect that all of his obligations had been met. When notice was posted that the legislature had prohibited this practice the Six Companies posted a counterblast:

If anyone does not pay what has been expended, the companies will get out a warrant and arrest him and deliver him over to the American courts, and then if the Chinaman loses his baggage and passage ticket it will not be any concern of the companies.[12]

Whatever the actual conditions may have been, appearances convinced the average Californian that in the Chinese laborer he was meeting competition that had many of the earmarks of slavery. And the Civil War was altogether too recent to make those earmarks attractive.

No charge against the Chinese was made more frequently nor with more sympathetic hearing than that relating to their low standard of living. Practically all of the Chinese laborers in California were single men and lived in very restricted quarters. In most cases they came, not to settle permanently, but to accumulate an amount sufficient to enable them to return to China and live in comparative comfort. Accustomed to living on a few cents a day, with the higher wage scale in California the laborer hoped to be able to attain his goal in a relatively short time, even with the increased cost of supplies. Hence, ". . . . they work on patiently for years, saving every cent, living cheaply and working cheaply."[13]

Those who opposed Chinese cheap labor urged that the American laborer, with his ideal of a home and family, could not compete with the Chinese because he could not live on the Chinese level of wages. Hence, American immigrants, so greatly desired in California, would not come, or if they came, would not stay. Comparisons were made with Gresham's Law of money, and with conditions in the south, where free labor was unable and unwilling to compete with slave labor. As a sample of outside opinion concerning California labor conditions the *Denver News* was quoted, "Give California a wide berth, for the laborer is not worthy of his hire in that state, even when there is work for him to do."[14] The presence of Chinese laborers was held responsible for an

---

[12]*Bulletin*, Oct. 11, 13, 1883. In 1880 appeal was made to the State Board of Equalization to tax the Six Companies for their alleged assets in these contracts. *Chronicle*, July 25, 1880.
[13]Sacramento *Bee*, April 4, 1876. This is from a statement by the Chinese themselves. See also Gibson, *Chinese in America*, 36.
[14]*Chronicle*, April 2, 1876. Butte *Record*, July 1, 1876. *Bulletin*, Nov. 18, 1876, *Post*, June 14, 1878.

increasing number of "hoodlums" among the young men of California, because the Chinese preempted the opportunities for finding work, and their wage scale degraded labor to a level so low that white boys would not engage in it. At the same time commodity prices to the consumer were not lowered.[15]

Many employers welcomed the Chinese laborer because his low wage scale enabled them to inaugurate undertakings which otherwise might not have been able to compete with the older establishments in the east. Others claimed that white labor was not available, while some insisted that the Chinese created additional labor for the whites, of a higher grade than that done by the Chinese. This was one phase of the question on which California disagreed with the east. Postmaster General Key, after a visit to California, spoke very highly of Chinese laborers. "It is wonderful to see how little a Chinaman can live on." What was, perhaps, a common view in the east was:

> If the people of California were capable of viewing their own interest without passion or prejudice, they would perceive they have a great advantage over the rest of the country in the cheapness of Chinese labor. It favors a rapid development of the resources of that wonderful state. It enables them to undersell in all markets every exportable article which their soil, climate and mineral wealth enable them to produce.[16]

Especially irritating to opponents of the Chinese were the statements of easterners, on the basis of very meagre information, belittling the problem of Chinese labor. When President Anderson of Chicago University and Henry Ward Beecher, after short visits to California, gave lectures and interviews deriding the opposition to the Chinese and accusing Californians of gross exaggeration regarding the danger from Chinese immigration, the press answered with bitter denunciation. The *Post,* which was probably the most radical anti-Chinese newspaper in the state, said,

> It is difficult to preserve good temper in the face of such balderdash from such a source. This sensational word monger (Beecher) taunts us with the theory of evolution, and twittingly declares that if least fitted to survive, then we should go to the wall. . . . . But only let the general government release our people from federal obligations, and with our own state laws and local enactments we will free ourselves from the leprous evil, or, failing in that, with the same right arms that founded this western empire, will prove to the world that the imperial Saxon race, though but a million strong, can maintain its claim even against four hundred million serfs to possess and forever hold untrammeled the fair continent of America. . . . . The silence of the grave would be all that would tell of the China-man's existence here.[17]

Many Californians opposed Chinese labor because it represented

[15]*Call,* Aug. 29, 1877, Feb. 2, 1879. *Alta,* Jan. 23, 1874. *Report 689,* 81, 246, 322, 352, 356.
[16]*Call,* March 27, 1879. Key's statement, *Call,* Nov. 1, 2, 1878. *Report 689,* 516-558, *et passim.*
[17]*Post,* March 19, 1879. See also *Chronicle,* April 2, 1876. *Call,* Oct. 7, 1878. *Bulletin,* April 3, 1876. *Post,* April 3, 1876, June 29, Sept. 24, 1878.

a standard upon which no European could live. As one writer insisted, the Chinese were denounced, not because they sold their labor cheaply, but because their civilization was such that they *could* sell cheaply. In other words, Californians objected to the Chinese because they were willing to be the mudsills of society.[18] And it was considered a turn in the tide when an eastern writer pointed out that the reason why the white laborers could not compete with the Chinese was that the standard of living of the whites made larger and more diverse requirements than the narrow range of wants of the Chinese, and that "the survival of the fittest" was not a valid argument; one might just as well argue the superiority of the Canadian thistle because it overcomes useful grasses.[19]

This phase of the working of a low standard of living was not appreciated by all Californians. Some of those who favored their employment claimed that Chinese cheap labor had an effect very much like that of machinery, apparently depriving men of work but actually providing more jobs. This argument was opposed by Henry George. He insisted that "the essential thing about Chinese laborers is that they are cheap laborers." While the principal effect of labor-saving machinery is on production, increasing and cheapening it, the effect of cheap labor is chiefly on distribution. With cheap labor production remains practically the same, but the laborer has less purchasing power. Actually, the higher labor is, the more efficient it is likely to be. Thus cheap labor may even raise the cost of production, since there may be less units produced, due both to the lower efficiency and to the lower purchasing power of cheap labor.[20] George's argument was too involved to become a popular one, but even the ordinary citizen could see the force of his statement that the cheap laborer compels other laborers to work cheaply.

This cheap labor made an insidious appeal to Californians because it offered comforts at small cost and relief from the unusually high prices of white labor. Many even of those opposed to the Chinese patronized them. William Wellock, one of Denis Kearney's lieutenants, charged that the product of the more than ten thousand Chinese cigarmakers in San Francisco was being consumed, not by Stanford, Crocker, Flood and other wealthy men, but by the workingmen. Asserting that the Chinese came and remained because Californians were profiting by their presence, editors complained:

> The Chinaman is here because his presence pays, and he will remain and continue to increase so long as there is money in him. When the time comes that he is no longer profitable *that* generation will take care of him and will send him

[18]*Argonaut*, Dec. 29, 1877. See also the issues of Oct. 27, Nov. 3, 10, 17, Dec. 1, 1877.
[19]*Bulletin*, May 9, 1878, quoting from M. J. Dee, "Chinese Immigration," *North American Review*, May-June, 1878, 506-526.
[20]*Report 689*, 276-281, 541, 556, 667. *Post*, July 15, 1878.

back. We will not do it so long as the pockets into which the profit of his labor flows continue to be those appertaining to our pantaloons.

They do not go because the people of California, while protesting against their presence, continue to utilize their labor in a hundred ways. In this matter private interest dominates public interest.[21]

The decades of most intensive anti-Chinese agitation were burdened with problems of railroad, land, and other monopolies, and anything smacking of monopoly was certain to arouse instant antagonism. Californians saw in the Chinese a developing monopoly of sinister mien. As they entered one field of activity after another it was claimed that they not only drove out American laborers but also tended to monopolize the industry. This was charged particularly in regard to cigar and shoe making and certain types of garment manufacture. They were credited with great imitative skill, and it was claimed that the only industry into which the Chinese had gone without monopolizing it was that of woolen manufacture, and that this was due to the large amount of capital required. "Where little capital is required, there the Mongol is sure to triumph."[22]

When eastern interests objected to the anti-Chinese agitation on the ground that it would injure our trade opportunities in China, Californians replied that this trade was very one-sided. Figures were quoted showing that our exports to China in 1878 totaled more than $23,000,000 and our imports over $18,000,000, but that some $16,000,000 of our exports were in gold and silver bullion, very largely remittances by Chinese in California, covering not only about five millions in savings, but also purchases of Chinese goods. It was charged that the Chinese purchased most of their food and clothing in China, and that factories for the duplication of American goods were being set up in China.

We may sell them samples of goods, but in a short period they will make goods as good as the sample. . . . . It is not at all improbable that within twenty years we shall find the East demanding protection from Chinese cheap labor in China as loudly as California now demands protection from the same kind of labor within her own limits. The fundamental fact of this question is that at home or abroad the Chinese can produce cheaper than any other people in existence.[23]

The Chinese were charged with contributing to monopoly in connection with the great landholders and the railroads. The latter had received large grants from the government, while the former had acquired the Spanish and Mexican holdings, and were included in the general anti-monopoly agitation. Since these landed interests were among the most ardent advocates of continued Chinese immigration the charge

[21]Sacramento *Record-Union*, Jan. 10, 1879. *News Letter*, April 1, 1876. See also *Chronicle*, June 1, 1878. *Report 689*, 399, 424, 622.
[22]*Bulletin*, March 27, 1876. See also Stockton *Independent*, April 12, 1876, *Report 689*, 80, 104, 244-247, 554, *et passim*.
[23]*Call*, Oct. 18, 1879. See also *Bulletin*, Aug. 7, 1879, July 22, 1882. *Chronicle*, April 27, 1873, March 15, 1879. *Post*, July 27, 1878. Hittell, *California*, IV, 101.

was frequently voiced that California was in danger of having a "caste system of lords and serfs" foisted upon it, the great holders of land and the railroads being represented as "Chinese emigration bureaus" and the largest "Chinese employment offices" on the coast. The anti-Chinese element in California looked upon these "monopolists" as among the chief mainstays of the Chinese. The claim of eastern newspapers that the "better class" of Californians favored the Chinese was answered with,

> Nobody is in favor of anything of the kind but the cormorants, desert-grabbers and other Judas Iscariots of their race, who would sell the whole land—people, liberties, institutions and all—for their own private aggrandizement. . . . .[24]

These great landowners were regarded as worse than the plantation owners of slave days. The only way to solve the situation was to break up the large holdings into small farms. "The Mongolian will be ground out with the growth of genuine American circumstances." When J. C. G. Kennedy appeared in Washington on behalf of the Chinese Six Companies and of the "agricultural interests" of California, it was alleged that he had been connected with the slave interest before the Civil War and that President Lincoln had removed him from office because of his activities in this cause. His actions were denounced.

> It is the nearest to an open declaration upon the part of the Mexican grant-holders of California of a deliberate purpose to make a struggle for 'Chinese cheap labor' that has yet come to our notice. The great landowners are evidently on the warpath.[25]

From an economic viewpoint employers and those seeking employment differed widely concerning the effect of the Chinese in the state. With few exceptions employers considered them beneficial as a flexible supply of labor, cheap, submissive, and efficient; but those whose only capital was their ability to work were almost unanimous in the opinion that the Chinese were highly detrimental to the best interests of the state. Each group saw the problem through the spectacles of its own economic interests.

Of scarcely less frequent mention in the opposition to the Chinese were charges concerning their morals. Like all frontier societies, California was not distinguished for its devotion to religious and moral ideals, but this did not prevent the most severe strictures upon immoral practices of a different sort. One of the leaders against the Chinese declared,

> . . . . their moral condition is as bad and degraded as four thousand years of heathenism can make it, and . . . . their physical condition is as low as the practice of all the crimes that have been known since history was written can make it.[26]

---

[24]*Chronicle*, Jan. 2, 1877. *Alta*, July 6, 1857, Dec. 17, 1877. *Argonaut*, Dec. 29, 1877. *Call*, Jan. 21, 1878. *Cong. Record*, 44th Cong., 1st sess., 2856. *Report 689*, 767-794.
[25]*Post*, March 22, 1878. See also *Post*, Feb. 14, Dec. 1, 1877, Jan. 15, Feb. 15, 24, 1878, Aug. 18, 1879. *Bulletin*, Feb. 15, 19, 1878, July 5, 31, Aug. 3, 1879. *Chronicle*, May 31, 1877.
[26]*Report 689*, 15. Pixley usually brought the questioning around to the moral effect of the Chinese in California.

In some cases the charge against the Chinese was simply that they were dishonest and unreliable, and that the entire business life of China was permeated by the idea that every person who handled a transaction should take his share of graft. More specifically, they were accused of having no regard for the sanctity of an oath. As early as 1854 legislation was proposed forbidding Chinese testimony against whites, and while it did not pass, a decision of the state supreme court during the year accomplished the same purpose. Several later attempts to admit Chinese testimony were defeated, and this attitude was urged by Pacific coast senators with such force in 1870 as to prevent their admission to naturalization.[27] Of like character was the charge of falsifying tax records. Numerous instances were cited to show the smuggling of Chinese immigrants and the violation or evasion of internal revenue and poll tax laws.[28]

Of the other vices charged to the Chinese those of opium smoking and gambling were outstanding. Opium dens were numerous in San Francisco, but since the effect of smoking was quieting, the addicts did not come in conflict with the police as did inebriated whites. However, when white people began to frequent the opium resorts more notice was taken of them. Games of chance seem to have been the chief means of excitement and recreation for the Chinese. At one time it was claimed that there were in San Francisco Chinatown more than one hundred fan-tan games and nine organized lottery companies with three hundred agencies and two drawings daily, patronized by thousands of both whites and Chinese. This situation had been in existence for years, and the police were accused of conniving with the gambling element. The police, however, declared that since gambling was a natural passion with the Chinese, they would evade any legal restriction; that gambling was being carried on behind barred doors, and that it was almost impossible for a white man to enter.[29]

No phase of the Chinese question attracted more attention than that of prostitution. It was charged that there was not a single home, in the American sense, among all of the Chinese on the coast, and that of the four thousand Chinese women in the state all were either prostitutes or concubines. It was generally charged, also, that these women were purchased, kidnapped, or lured by panderers in China, brought to America under contract, and sold to Chinese men, either as concubines or for

[27]*Cong. Globe,* 41st Cong., 2d sess., 5123-5125, 5177. *Report 689,* 119, 1022. *Bulletin,* April 10, May 22, 1857, Jan. 17, April 9, 1862, April 27, 1882. *Alta,* March 10, 12, 26, 1854. Hittell, *California,* IV, 111-112.

[28]*Alta,* Feb. 11, 1871. *Bulletin,* Oct. 15, 16, 25, Nov. 13, 15, 19, 20, 1883, Jan. 7, 1884, May 18, 1887. *Report 689,* 996, 1129.

[29]*Report 689,* 187, 223, 403. Drunkenness was very uncommon among them. *Ibid.,* 89, 668. *Post,* June 2, Aug. 9, 16, 20, Sept. 10, 1879. *Call,* Sept. 28, 1878. *Chronicle,* July 15, 16, 1877, Sept. 15, 1878.

professional prostitution. "They are bought and sold like slaves at the will of their masters."[30] Apparently this traffic began quite early. Frequent protests were made against the practice and against the conditions attending it, and on one occasion the heads of the Chinese Companies offered their assistance in curbing the traffic. The Page Act of 1875 was thought to have stopped it, but within a few years an extensive system of smuggling was unearthed.[31]

On first consideration one might regard the moral and religious phase of this question as insignificant, since it is hardly true that Chinese practices were "worse" than those of Californians. But the methods of the Chinese were different, and this fact alone was enough to make them an object of attack. To Californians the immoralities of the Chinese seemed to be an integral part of their way of living, ingrained through many centuries of practice, rather than an occasional excursion into a by-path. As a contemporary writer expressed it,

They live in close quarters, not coarsely filthy like ignorant and besotted Irish, but bearing a savor of inherent and refined uncleanliness that is almost more disgusting. Their whole civilization impresses me as a low, disciplined, perfected, sensuous sensualism. Everything in their life and their habits seems cut and dried like their food. There is no sign of that abandonment to an emotion, to a passion, good or bad, that marks the western races. . . . . . The whole matter of the Chinese religion seems very negative and inconclusive; and apparently it has little hold upon them. There is no fanaticism in it,—no appreciable degree of earnestness about it.[32]

Opposition on the basis of religion, however, was not directed primarily against the religious beliefs of the Chinese. The religious question was raised chiefly as a reaction to the attitude of the Protestant churches toward restrictive legislation. The movement against the Chinese came during a period of great missionary activity on the part of most of the American churches, and several denominations had undertaken work among the Chinese, both on the coast and in China. The church leaders feared that the anti-Chinese agitation would have an adverse effect upon this work. Their utterances, resolutions, and memorials to Congress opposing measures for the restriction of Chinese immigration elicited bitter criticism from the California press, both for their utterances and for their missionary endeavors. When eastern Methodists sent memorials against the Fifteen Passenger Bill to President Hayes, the *Post*

. . . . [protested] most emphatically against the criminal recklessness of religious fanaticism in the East in its bearing upon the Chinese question. . . . . The Chinese,

---

[30]*Report 689*, 405. On this subject religious leaders agreed very closely with the anti-Chinese leaders. As part of his testimony Gibson presented his translations of two bills of sale, contracts under which Chinese women were imported. See Gibson, *Chinese in America*, 139-157. Condit, *The Chinaman As We See Him*, 144-155.

[31]*Bulletin*, Nov. 26, 29, Dec. 6, 13, 14, 15, 16, 19, 20, 1887, Sept. 26, Oct. 3, 1889, March 13, 1890. *Alta*, April 25, 26, 1854, Sept. 14, 1867, Jan. 16, 18, 1870. *Overland Monthly*, April 1869, 344 f.

[32]Samuel Bowles, *Our New West*, Hartford, 1869, 407.

whether they profess Christianity or not, remain at heart worshipers of their ancestors. This is their religion, and none other. . . . . Our opinion is that the time, money and effort wasted on Chinese missions could be turned to very much better account among our own people.[33]

The religious forces on the coast, however, were not unanimous in favoring unrestricted immigration. The first voices of dissent were those of Roman Catholic priests. Gradually disaffection made its appearance among the Protestants. A representative of one of the more liberal groups criticised an eastern religious paper for calling the agitation against the Chinese "a crazy labor reform movement, headed by Kearney and the hoodlums of San Francisco," because the evil effects of the Chinese made it a much larger question than this. However, "we must strike while the iron is hot even if Denis Kearney is blowing the bellows." Even the Methodists, who were generally regarded as the chief opponents of restriction, displayed tendencies toward a change of attitude. Some of the most prominent leaders took a decided stand against the further immigration of the Chinese. The most notable religious declaration against the Chinese, however, was that of S. V. Blakeslee before the State Association of Congregational Churches in 1877, in which he compared the conditions in California with those under slavery in the south. Thus, while eastern religious defenders of the Chinese were irritating California restrictionists, religious leaders on the coast tended more and more to oppose unrestricted immigration.[34]

No one source furnished such unfailing inspiration for criticism of the Chinese, especially from the social and political viewpoint, as the evils of Chinatown. No matter when nor how often the need might arise, a short tour of Chinatown would supply ample material for any amount or degree of condemnation. Within four years of statehood a committee reported this district overcrowded, the houses filthy beyond imagination, pervaded by a "stench almost insupportable," numerous sick in every dwelling, excessive fire hazards due to inadequate cooking facilities, the women all prostitutes and the men inveterate gamblers. Later reports on Chinatown were elaborations of this one, as may be seen from that of the health inspectors in 1870:

All through the dark and dingy garrets and cellars, steaming with air breathed over and over, and filled with the fumes of opium, they groped their way with candle in hand and hanging on to their official noses until they found a door or window where they could procure a fresh breath of air. Rooms, which would be considered close quarters for a single white man, were occupied by shelves a foot and a half wide, placed one above another on all sides of the room, and on these

[33]Post, Feb. 22, Nov. 4, 1879. See also Sacramento Record-Union, Oct. 7, 1878, Feb. 24, 1879. Chronicle, Oct. 7, 8, Nov. 24, 1878, June 27, 1879, April 3, 6, 7, 10, 1890. Presbyterians, Baptists, Methodists, Congregationalists, and Episcopalians carried on missionary work among the Chinese in California.
[34]Blakeslee's address is in Cal. Senate, Chinese Immigration, 239-249. It was excerpted by numerous newspapers. For other groups see Alta, Feb. 26, 1873. Post, Jan. 8, 1877, April 2, 1879. Unitarian Advocate, April, 1879.

from twenty to forty Chinamen are stowed away to sleep. In many of these places there is scarcely a chance for even a breath of fresh air to creep in, and the occupants are obliged to breathe over and over again the limited allowance. How life can exist in such a place is a mystery. Besides being crowded in the manner above stated, in many of the lodging-houses filth has been allowed to accumulate to the depth of several inches, and in a number of instances the moisture, leach-like, was found dripping from rooms above. In the cellars and underground coops, which frequently extend back half a block, there is no way to obtain a circulation of air —all that does creep in being by the narrow door of the street. Here they burn oil lamps and cook their food, the smoke from which fills the air, and curls lazily up out of the door when it chances to be open.[35]

Sporadic attempts were made to remedy or remove the evil, but instead Chinatown expanded and similar conditions were reported in other cities, until it was said, "The overcrowding of Chinatown is productive of more evils than any other habit of these semi-barbarians."[36]

In addition to the stench, filth, crowding, and general dilapidation with which Chinatown was accused of afflicting the community, another serious charge was made that the Chinese were introducing foreign diseases among the whites. For instance, it was claimed by both civil and medical authorities that Chinese men and women were afflicted with venereal disease to an uncommon degree. The Chinese prostitutes were accused of luring young boys into their houses and of infecting them with the disease. A medical journal charged that the blood stream of the Anglo-Saxon population was being poisoned through the American men who, "by thousands nightly," visited these resorts.[37] A cause of rather frequent concern to the officials were outbreaks of smallpox. The Chinese were suspected as the source of the disease, since cases appeared among them while they were still on shipboard. They were condemned especially for not reporting their cases of the disease. "It (Chinatown) is almost invariably the seed-bed of smallpox, whence the scourge is sent abroad into the city."[38]

The most exciting charge under this head, however, was that the Chinese were introducing leprosy into California. The very strangeness of the disease made this charge all the more ominous. It was claimed that wherever Chinese coolies had gone leprosy had developed, and that purchasers of Chinese goods were likely to contract the disease. Dr. Charles C. O'Donnell, a politically minded physician, discovered a case in a Chinese washhouse, placed him in an express wagon and drove through the streets, haranguing the crowds on the street corners con-

[35]*Alta*, May 16, 1870. The earlier report, *Alta*, Aug. 22, 1854.
[36]*Bulletin*, Sept. 2, 1885. For some of these efforts see *Bulletin*, Aug. 29, Sept. 3, 7, 1878, July 21, 1880. The Canadian Commission of 1884 reported, "There is no question that the Chinese quarters are the filthiest and most disgusting places in Victoria, overcrowded hotbeds of disease and vice." Quoted by Campbell, *Chinese Coolie Emigration*, 42.
[37]*Chronicle*, Nov. 20, and *Post*, Nov. 21, 1876, quoting the San Francisco *Medico-Literary Journal*, Nov., 1876. See *Report 689*, 117, 131, 190, 1031.
[38]*Chronicle*, July 22, 1878. *Bulletin*, Jan. 29, 31, Feb. 5, 7, 1880, April 20, Dec. 21, 1881. *Report 689*, 127, 208.

cerning the dangers to which the community was being exposed. The contention of some physicians that it was not real leprosy but rather a "sporadic case of elephantiasis" did not help matters a great deal. During a period of less than ten years the Board of Supervisors of San Francisco arranged for the deportation of forty-eight cases.[39]

What many considered the most fundamental objection to the Chinese was their difference from Americans in racial characteristics and their unwillingness to adopt American customs and ideals. Some felt that the difficulty was merely superficial, and that if the Chinese would adopt western garb and mingle with Americans the most bitter prejudices against them would disappear. Others, however, were convinced that the difference was much deeper, holding that the Chinese civilization had crystallized and that they could not assimilate with the American people. Even if no natural barrier existed, the Chinese were so devoted to their native land that, in case of death in this country, their bones were to be returned to China. It was claimed that they showed no inclination to make this country their permanent home nor to become citizens; indeed, it was felt that they were not fitted to become citizens, for they were imbued with monarchistic ideals and would become the tools of bosses.[40]

Considering all of these factors it is not surprising that the leaders of the movement against the Chinese should claim to see in the situation a great struggle between Asiatic and American ideals and civilizations. It may be called race prejudice, but race prejudice is not instinctive. It generally has an economic or social basis, a fear due to a lower standard of living or to a higher standard of effort. One editor expressed it during the heat of the agitation:

We have won this glorious land inch by inch from the red man in vain; we have beaten back the legions of George the Third for nothing; we have suppressed rebellion and maintained the integrity of our country for no good purpose whatsoever, if we are now to surrender it to a horde of Chinese, simply because they are so degraded that they can live on almost nothing, and underbid our own flesh and blood in the labor market. The people of California cannot endure it.[41]

It is of interest here to note that the Chinese were not the first, as they were not the last, against whom such statements were directed. Just as the American frontier has had a tendency to repeat itself across the country, so agitation against the influx of new racial groups has recurred in our history. A generation before the agitation against the Chinese it was said of the Irish that "they do more work for less money than the native workingman, and live on a lower standard, thereby decreasing wages."

The foreigners in general retained their pride for the fatherland and associated together in clannish exclusiveness, forming their own secret societies, which were

[39]*Municipal Reports, 1884-1885*, Appendix, 234. *Post*, Nov. 19, 1877, Aug. 20, Sept. 20, 1878. See *Bulletin*, Sept. 19, 1878, April 18, 1890.
[40]*Report 689*, 16, 103, 188, 543-544, 586-587, 678-679, et al.
[41]*Marin Journal*, April 13, 1876.

sometimes political, and even their own military companies. In addition, they constituted a source of political evil with citizenship often illegally conferred upon them and as the ignorant tools of corrupt politicians in innumerable election frauds.[42]

If we place beside this California's official declaration concerning the Chinese the comparison is obvious:

> During their entire settlement in California they have never adapted themselves to our habits, modes of dress, or our educational system, have never learned the sanctity of an oath, never desired to become citizens, or to perform the duties of citizenship, never discovered the difference between right and wrong, never ceased the worship of their idol gods, or advanced a step beyond the musty traditions of their native hive. Impregnable to all the influences of our Anglo-Saxon life, they remain the same stolid Asiatics that have floated on the rivers and slaved in the fields of China for thirty centuries of time.[43]

These, then, constituted California's indictment against the Chinese. Most important was economic competition, with its threat of the degradation of labor and the intrenchment of monopoly. Chinese moral and religious practices differed from those of Americans and seemed ingrained and unchangeable. Racial differences, the apparent unconcern for American political and social institutions, and the clannishness which produced the inevitable "Chinatown" served as constant and never-failing sources of complaint. By the frequent reiteration of these charges Californians convinced themselves and their neighbors, and finally the United States, that an effective remedy must be found.

[42]Arthur C. Cole, "Nativism in the Lower Mississippi Valley," *Mississippi Valley Historical Review*, VI, 260-261. See also Stephenson, "Nativism in the Forties and Fifties," *Ibid.*, IX, 185-202. The statement regarding the Irish is from Henry Pratt Fairchild, *Immigration*, 69, quoting *North American Review*, Jan., 1841.
[43]Cal. Senate, *Chinese Immigration*, 63. (Memorial to Congress).

CHAPTER III

CALIFORNIA ANTI-CHINESE AGITATION PRIOR TO 1876

THE MOVEMENT against the Chinese in California owed much to fortuitous circumstance and to the operation of a philosophy of opportunism, both economic and political. Without these factors the struggle for exclusion would have been longer and much more difficult. This statement, however, should not cause us to overlook the conscious effort and organization of definite groups for the express purpose of achieving a recognized objective. And of all the groups interested in securing the restriction of Chinese immigration none was more conspicuous than organized labor.

Centering in San Francisco, labor organizations appeared within a few years after statehood. Most of the trades were organized during the first decade, but continuity was not achieved until after the Civil War. Taking advantage of a close election, in 1868 the labor groups achieved an eight-hour day and a mechanics' lien law. But their success was only temporary. Employers resisted the shorter day; the completion of the Central Pacific Railroad released thousands of men, unorganized; the panic of 1873 dislocated industry, while jealousies among the trades prevented united effort. In their desperation they organized the Workingmen's Party of California in 1877, which disappeared within five years, with the return of prosperity. Laboring men continued to work together, however, under such leadership as the Representative Assembly of Trades and Labor Unions, the Knights of Labor, the International Workingmen's Associations, the Federated Trades of the Pacific Coast, and finally, the Sate Federation of Labor.[1]

The growth of organized labor has been very closely connected with the movement against Chinese immigration.

> This long camping in front of what was felt to be a common enemy has contributed more than any other one factor to the strength of the California labor movement. . . . . It is the one subject upon which there has never been the slightest difference of opinion, the one measure on which it has always been possible to obtain concerted action. . . . . Legislation prohibiting the further immigration of Oriental laborers has been the chief object of the organized activities of the working people of California for over fifty years.[2]

In seeking to accomplish this objective almost every possible form of propaganda was employed, from parades, conventions, and boycotts to political bargaining, and even the formation of a separate political party. Very frequently labor organizations were joined by other groups, not

---

[1] Eaves, *California Labor Legislation*, 1-81. This work is such a complete and thorough study of organized labor in California and its relation to the Chinese that only the most important phases will be treated in this chapter.
[2] *Ibid.*, 6, 105.

always by invitation. Sometimes these took the form of anti-coolie clubs or other secret associations, or merely unattached mobs of camp followers, who always added heat and noise to the movement, but seldom clarified the problem or made the solution easier.

Organized labor, however, might have been powerless against the Chinese except for the peculiar political situation which developed. During the period of this agitation the political parties in the state were so nearly equal in strength that, except for the first six years of statehood, no political party was able to elect its candidate for governor more than twice in succession, and often by majorities of less than one thousand votes. Under these circumstances the labor forces, unified and keenly alive to the situation, held the balance of power. Political leaders, to whom convictions on the merits of Chinese immigration were secondary to the winning of elections, found themselves driven to the advocacy of restriction. These two factors, the balance between political parties and the unanimity of organized labor in opposition to Chinese immigration, interacted upon each other to bring about restrictive legislation. Organized labor utilized the rivalry between political parties to attain its ends, while the political parties seized upon the Chinese question to capture the labor vote. Because of these conditions there is a certain amount of truth in the statement that legislative resolutions did not represent the real convictions of the legislators, and that party platforms were little more than bait thrown to the masses. The politician and the anti-Chinese agitator fitted into each other's purposes, but the implication that politics and race prejudice were practically the sole causes of the movement is not warranted by the evidence.[3]

The earliest legislative action against the Chinese was connected with the taxation of foreign miners, a policy begun by the first legislature and continued for almost two decades. When gold was discovered prospectors came from every part of the world. An unusually large number came from the Latin American countries, from northern Mexico to Chile. Opposition to these groups developed because previous experience made them superior producers, because of race prejudice, and because they carried a large portion of their earnings out of the country. The Chinese suffered along with the others. In 1850 all miners who were not native-born citizens of the United States or had not become citizens under the treaty of Guadeloupe Hidalgo were required to take out licenses for which they must pay twenty dollars a month. Failure to do so was punishable by expulsion from the mines, with possible fine and imprisonment. It is significant to note, however, that this law was directed primarily against miners from Chile, Mexico, and Australia, and that

---

[3]Coolidge, *Chinese Immigration*, 67. *Report 689*, 702-709, 922-925. Davis, *Political Conventions*, 288, 430, 532, 594.

the "Chinean" miners are mentioned only as one of several groups working for others. This law was upheld by the state supreme court, but because of difficulties connected with its enforcement it was repealed the following year.[4]

In 1852 the large increase in Chinese immigration and an obvious attempt to introduce the coolie system made anti-foreign legislation a pressing question. Mass meetings protested the efforts of "certain ship owners, capitalists and merchants, to flood the State with degraded Asiatics," a "Committee of Vigilance" was formed, and Chinese property was burned. Senator Tingley's bill to make enforcible in California contracts made in China was defeated, the debate bringing forth many of the "coolie" charges which became so common in the agitation of a later day. The result was a new tax on foreign miners of three dollars a month, employers being made liable for the tax.[5] The Assembly in 1853 received from its special committee on the Chinese an extensive report, especially on the "Chinese Companies." As a result the tax was increased to four dollars a month, and elaborate provisions were inserted for the efficient collection of the tax, including authority to the collector to seize and sell the property of the person failing to pay the tax. The law was ordered printed in the Chinese language, as well as in French and Spanish.[6]

In 1855 occurred the greatest excitement on the Chinese question of the entire decade. A miners' convention in Shasta county complained that the Chinese had usurped all of the placers, and predicted that if their coming were not prohibited at once there would follow scenes of bloodshed that would bring disgrace upon the state. Concerning the evils due to the presence of the Chinese the majority and minority reports of the select committee appointed by the two houses differed only in degree. Even then the relation of Chinese immigration to Oriental trade was recognized. The Assembly majority declared, "We want the Chinese *trade,* but we do not want her surplus *population.*" They insisted that the direct question involved was that of the Chinese laborer and the capitalist versus the American laborer.

> The American laborer claims the *exclusive privilege* and *right* of occupying and working the immense placers of our State. . . . . If this class of foreigners are excluded from the mines, our own laboring classes will for a long series of years have the advantage of capitalists. Our laborers wish to keep up the value of their toil to a fair standard of competition *among themselves,* but you allow capitalists

---

[4]*Cal. Statutes, 1850,* 221-223. *Senate Journal, 1850,* Appendix, 493-497; *Ibid., 1851,* 315. *People v. Naglee,* 1 California, 232.
[5]*Cal. Statutes, 1852,* 84. *Senate Journal, 1852,* 15, 67-68, 192, 217, 306-307, 372-378, 669-675, 731-737. Governor Bigler sent the first of his three messages against the Chinese. *Appendix to the Legislative Journals, 1852,* 829. Answered by the Chinese, *Living Age,* vol. 34, pp. 32-34, July 3, 1852.
[6]*Cal. Statutes, 1853,* 62-63, 82. *Assembly Journal, 1853,* Appendix, Doc. 28. See also *Senate Journal, 1854,* 574-576, 643.

to import Chinese labor upon them, and the equilibrium is destroyed, capital is triumphant, and the laboring poor of America must submit to the unholy sacrifice.[7]

This committee recommended that all persons of foreign birth who were ineligible to citizenship should be excluded from the privilege of working the mines of the state. But when the minority pointed out the possible ill effects of this sort of legislation upon our trade with China, and also that some counties would suffer from the loss in miners' tax revenue, it was enacted that the license tax should be continued at four dollars a month until October, 1855, be increased to six dollars a month for the following year, and that the monthly rate should be increased two dollars each succeeding year. Foreigners who declared their intention of becoming citizens were exempted from paying the tax.[8] This act, however, created a great deal of dissatisfaction, and the following year the old rate of four dollars was restored. Three subsequent legislatures adopted additional regulations for the enforcement of this law. By 1868 the income from this tax had been greatly reduced, largely because the Chinese were turning to other occupations, and the entire matter was turned over to the counties.[9]

In addition to the tax on foreign miners an effort was made in 1855 to prevent the Chinese from entering California. Any ship bringing into the state persons ineligible to become citizens was required to pay a tax of fifty dollars for each such passenger. If the tax were not paid within three days the Commissioner of Emigrants was to bring suit for the amount due, which was to constitute a lien against the ship. This act, however, was declared unconstitutional by the state supreme court, on the ground that the power of Congress to regulate commerce is an exclusive power. Shortly afterward, in spite of this adverse decision, the legislature enacted that no Chinese or Mongolian should be permitted to enter the state, under penalty of both fine and imprisonment for those in charge of any ship violating this law.[10]

In 1862 occurred another of the early outbursts against the Chinese. During the preceding two years there had been a noticeable increase in the number of arrivals, and the first anti-coolie club, of which there were many in later years, was formed at this time. The demand for further legislation was voiced first of all by Governor Stanford in his inaugural address:

To my mind it is clear, that the settlement among us of an inferior race is to be discouraged by every legitimate means. Asia, with her numberless millions,

---

[7]*Assembly Journal, 1855*, Appendix. See also *Senate Journal, 1855*, 50-54, 298. *Daily Herald*, Feb. 16, 1855.
[8]*Senate Journal, 1855*, Appendix, Docs. 16 and 19. *Cal. Statutes, 1855*, 216-217.
[9]*Cal. Statutes, 1856*, 141. *Ibid., 1857*, 182-183. *Ibid., 1858*, 302-303. *Ibid., 1861*, 447. *Ibid., 1867-68*, 173-174.
[10]*Cal. Statutes, 1855*, 194-195. *Ibid., 1858*, 295-296. 7 California, 169-171. This law had not been repealed in 1862. 20 California, 538.

sends to our shores the dregs of her population. Large numbers of this class are already here; and, unless we do something early to check their immigration, the question, which of the two tides of immigration, meeting upon the shores of the Pacific, shall be turned back, will be forced upon our consideration, when far more difficult than now of disposal. There can be no doubt but that the presence among us of numbers of degraded and distinct people must exercise a deleterious influence upon the superior race, and to a certain extent, repel desirable immigration. It will afford me great pleasure to concur with the Legislature in any constitutional action, having for its object the repression of the immigration of the Asiatic races.[11]

The Joint Select Committee of the legislature made a report which was quite favorable to the Chinese, and recommended that no further restrictions be placed upon their immigration. It was claimed that the fifty thousand Chinese in the state paid almost fourteen million dollars annually in taxes, licenses, duties, freights, and other charges, that their cheap labor would be of great value in developing the new industries of the state, and that the trade with China should be fostered. It was pointed out that treaty provisions and Supreme Court decisions deprived the state of authority to legislate against their coming.

Your committee is satisfied that there is no system of slavery or coolicism amongst the Chinese in this State. If there is any proof, going to establish the fact that any portion of the Chinese are imported into this State as slaves or coolies, your Committee have failed to discover it. . . . . Instead of driving them out of the State, bounties might be offered them to cultivate rice, tea, tobacco, and other articles. . . . . If a partial Providence has endowed us with ten talents, let us use them to gain other ten; and let us infuse into our benighted neighbors the blessings of that higher and purer civilization which we feel we were destined to establish over the whole earth.[12]

The Assembly, apparently not satisfied with this report, adopted a long memorial to Congress, stressing the evil effects of having a large number of unassimilable immigrants and the possible dangers of introducing a system of labor very similar to slavery. The admission by the Chinese merchants that there were only about one hundred respectable Chinese families in California was emphasized. Congress was urged to protect the coast against the further immigration of the Chinese, in order to avoid the dangers incident to the growing hostility toward them. This memorial failed of acceptance in the Senate, but two pieces of legislation were enacted. One was an amendment to a law of 1852, and required shipmasters to give a separate bond for each alien passenger. The other levied a monthly tax of two and a half dollars upon all Chinese, eighteen years of age or over, who were not already paying a license tax of some sort or who were not engaged in the production of rice, sugar, tea, or coffee. Collectors of this tax were authorized to seize and sell the property of those who refused to pay the tax.[13]

---

[11]*Senate Journal, 1862*, 99. This statement is interesting in the light of the subsequent importation of Chinese laborers for the Central Pacific Railroad, of which Stanford was president.
[12]*Appendix to the Journals of the Senate and Assembly, 1862*.
[13]*Cal. Statutes, 1862*, 462-465, 486. *Assembly Journal, 1862*, 544-550. Both acts were declared unconstitutional. 20 California, 534. 42 California, 578.

One of the most serious attacks upon the Chinese during this early period came, not from the legislature, but from the state supreme court. A man convicted of murder on the testimony of a Chinese witness appealed to the supreme court. The law provided that "No Black, or Mulatto person, or Indian shall be allowed to give evidence in favor of, or against a white man." Chief Justice Hugh C. Murray held that from the days of Columbus American Indians and Mongolians had been regarded as of the same human species; that the laws of California had been taken from those of other states, written when this belief was generally prevalent, and hence, that the law was intended to exclude all people of color from testifying in court against a white person. He added:

> We have carefully considered all the consequences resulting from a different construction, and are satisfied that, even in a doubtful case, we would be impelled to this decision on grounds of public policy. The same rule that would admit them to testify, would admit them to all the equal rights of citizenship, and we might soon see them at the polls, in the jury box, upon the bench and in our legislative halls.[14]

It is obvious that this decision opened the way for almost every sort of discrimination against the Chinese. Assault, robbery, and murder, to say nothing of lesser crimes, could be perpetrated against them with impunity, so long as no white person was available to witness in their behalf. Without a doubt this decision must bear a large part of the responsibility for the outrages committed against the Chinese. Efforts to amend the law so as to admit Chinese testimony were unsuccessful. Indeed, the law was amended to read, "No Indian, or person having one-half or more of Indian blood, or Mongolian, or Chinese, shall be permitted to give evidence against any white person." But following the Civil War this law was practically voided by the Civil Rights Act and the Fourteenth Amendment. It is true that the state supreme court handed down two decisions within one year upholding this law, but when the California codes were published two years later that part excluding Chinese testimony was omitted.[15]

In 1867 the Chinese question attained a position of outstanding importance in state politics, a position it was destined to maintain for almost forty years. That year the hatchet of party rivalry, camouflaged during the Civil War, was brought forth and sharpened anew, resulting in the disruption of the Union party. The labor groups were more strongly organized than ever before, with a definite list of demands, including legislation against Chinese immigration. The employment of Chinese

---

[14]*The People v. Hall*, 4 California, 399. Murray belonged to the American or Know Nothing Party. Bancroft speaks of him as "a man abandoned in character, immoral, venal, and thoroughly corrupt." *California Inter Pocula*, 605-607.
[15]*Code of Civil Procedure, 1872*, 493-494. For the Civil Rights Act provisions see *U. S. Statutes at Large, 1869-71*, 144, Secs. 16 and 17. The amendment is in *Cal. Statutes, 1863*, 69. The court decisions are in 36 California, 458-687, and 40 California, 198-221.

by the Central Pacific Railroad was at its peak, and the significance of their competition was becoming apparent. Anti-coolie clubs were increasing in number, a state association was formed, and mass meetings were held, declaring that "Every employer who substitutes Chinese labor for that of the citizen, is an enemy to the real prosperity of the State." Mob attacks became frequent and the newspapers began to take sides.[16]

To win the votes of these groups became a matter of vital importance to the political leaders. The Union convention nominated George C. Gorham, representing the "short hair" or Douglas wing of the party, and delivered itself of the general declaration,

That the importation of Chinese or any other people of the Mongolian race into the Pacific states or territories is in every respect injurious and degrading to American labor, by forcing it into unjust and ruinous competition, and an evil that should be restricted by legislation and abated by such legal and constitutional means as are in our power.

This indefinite statement, together with Gorham's avowed favor of Oriental trade and opposition to any strong measures against Chinese immigration, helped to bring about the election of Henry H. Haight, the Democratic candidate, whose platform and personal utterances called upon Congress to protect the Pacific states from the Chinese and urged the legislature to do all in its power to keep them out.[17] Throughout this period the tendency of the Republican party to favor the conservative and capitalistic interests inclined the labor groups toward the Democratic party, which usually took the stronger position against the Chinese. To California labor's view, land monopoly, capitalistic domination, and Chinese labor were all parts of one great evil.

One of the leading issues of the campaign of 1867 was the naturalization of the Chinese. Californians charged that they came merely to acquire a little money, after which they would return to their native land, and that they were utterly indifferent to American citizenship. At the same time, Californians were very much afraid that Congress would open the way for the Chinese to acquire citizenship. Gorham was accused of favoring the removal of the word "white" from the naturalization law, and his successful rival devoted a large part of his inaugural address to an attack upon the congressional policy of reconstruction. Both Democratic and Republican platforms declared opposition to admitting the Chinese to citizenship, the Democrats strongly condemning the Fifteenth Amendment on this ground. It is not surprising that both houses of the legislature rejected the Fifteenth Amendment by large

---

[16]*Alta*, March 7, 9, 10, 14, Sept. 14, 1867; March 4, Aug. 18, Dec. 22, 1868; Feb. 26, June 24, 1869. *Express*, March 7, 1867. *Sentinel*, March 30, 1867. Benjamin S. Brooks, *Appendix to the Opening Statement*, San Francisco, 1877.
[17]Davis, *Political Conventions*, 241-242, 249, 265, 267.

majorities. The uncertainty continued for several years, and there was widespread satisfaction when the Federal Circuit Court declared that under the naturalization laws the Chinese were not eligible to become citizens.[18]

In 1870 occurred the first of those spectacular demonstrations which became so common before the end of that decade. During the spring months numerous meetings of the unemployed were held. Among those who particularly felt the presence of the Chinese were the Knights of St. Crispin, an organization of shoemakers. With the cooperation of the Plumbers' and Carpenters' Eight Hour Leagues they promoted a great mass meeting in San Francisco. Preceding the meeting a monster parade was held, in which men carried transparencies bearing such messages as, "Women's Rights and no more Chinese Chambermaids," "Our Women are degraded by Coolie Labor," "No Servile Labor shall Pollute our Land," "American Trade Needs no Coolie Labor," "We want no Slaves or Aristocrats," and "The Coolie Labor System leaves us no Alternative— Starvation or Disgrace."

The leaders of this demonstration declared that its purpose was the beginning of an effort to rid California of Mongolians. A plan was presented for a state anti-Chinese convention, with the object

. . . . to oppose the immigration of Chinese laborers, and cultivate public opinion up to the abrogation of the treaty with China. . . . . We will not be content with anything short of an abrogation of the treaty with China except for commercial purposes.

The next day a written warning was sent to the heads of the Chinese Six Companies stating,

. . . . that we do not consider it just to us, or safe to the Chinamen to continue coming to the United States, and request them (the Companies) to give such notice to the public authorities of the Chinese Empire.[19]

In August the state anti-Chinese convention was held, the president stating that it was "the first Workingmen's Convention ever held." Numerous resolutions were adopted, condemning the coolie system, urging the abrogation of the Burlingame Treaty, the suppression of coolie immigration, and opposition to public officials employing Chinese and to subsidized steamer lines importing Chinese; repudiating all acts of violence against the Chinese, and calling upon the laboring classes of the United States to endorse these principles. The convention finally broke up into two factions, chiefly over the question of engaging in the San Francisco municipal election.[20] During this year the first indica-

[18]5 Sawyer, 155. *Alta*, Jan. 5, 1876, April 30, 1878; *Call*, April 18, 1877, May 10, 1878; *Chronicle*, April 18, 1877. Davis, *Political Conventions*, 290, 293. *Senate Journal, 1867-68*, 96-107; *1869-70*, 198-199, 245. *Assembly Journal, 1869-70*, 295-296. *Occident*, August 26, 1867.
[19]*Alta*, July 9, 16, 17, 1870. *Examiner*, July 9, 1870. Among the speakers were Henry George, Philip A. Roach, and A. M. Winn.
[20]*Alta*, Aug. 11, 12, 19, 24, 25, 31, Sept. 16, 1870.

tions of cooperation on the part of eastern labor groups were received, anti-Chinese meetings being held in Boston and New York. The interest of eastern laborers was being aroused by Henry George's strong article in the New York *Tribune* and by the shipping of Chinese to North Adams, Massachusetts, to break a strike of St. Crispins. With a view to increasing this interest the Mechanics' State Council sent a delegate to the National Labor Congress at Chicago.[21]

During the political campaign of 1871 occurred the first of the large-scale mob attacks on the Chinese, at Los Angeles on October twenty-fourth. The trouble originated in a feud between two Chinese companies over a Chinese woman said to belong to one of them and to have been stolen by the other. As usual in such affairs, very little damage resulted from the fighting between the two companies. The police arrested the participants, who were released on bail the next day. The fighting immediately was resumed. When the police intervened two officers were wounded and a civilian was killed. In a very few minutes a large mob rushed into the Chinese quarter, firing into houses, hanging those whom they caught alive, and appropriating all movable property. The entire affair lasted only four hours, but in that time at least eighteen persons were killed, several buildings were burned, and a large amount of loot was carried away.[22]

This event shocked the entire state, and in his inaugural address Governor Newton Booth condemned it in the most unsparing language. Its chief significance in the anti-Chinese agitation lay in its effect upon sentiment outside the state. Instances of violence became more frequent during the decade. When a particularly severe outbreak occurred at Chico the deepest concern was expressed over the hostile reaction sure to follow in the east toward the entire movement for restriction.

. . . . the escape of these villains would react most disastrously upon public sentiment throughout the East, and at Washington. All the efforts of the people of the Pacific Coast to secure limitation of Chinese immigration must be impotent so long as American brutality and barbarism are suffered to display themselves in this hideous fashion.[23]

The expected condemnation from outside the state was immediately forthcoming. The *Chronicle* printed quotations from a large number of eastern and middle western newspapers, adding, "The Chico butchery is bearing its humiliating fruit." It was with evident relish that the *Alta*

---

[21]*Alta*, July 11, Aug. 24, Oct. 12, 29, 1870. *Bulletin*, Nov. 10, 1870. New York *Tribune*, May 1, 1869.
[22]Los Angeles *Star*, Oct. 25, 26, 1871. *Alta*, Oct. 26, 1871. Cleland, *California*, 418. Chester P. Dorland, "The Chinese Massacre in Los Angeles," *Annual Publications* of the Historical Society of Southern California, III, Part II, 22-26. Bancroft, *California Inter Pocula*, 562-568. A somewhat different story is told by Horace Bell, *On the Old West Coast*, 166-177. See also Coolidge, *Chinese Immigration*, 261.
[23]Sacramento *Record-Union*, March 19, 1877. Governor Booth's statement is in *Senate Journal, 1871-72*, 115-116.

added to its account of the swift justice meted out to the perpetrators, "Will our Eastern brethren of the Press make a note of this?"[24]

While the campaign of 1873 was only for the election of members of the judiciary and of the legislature, and the chief interest concerned the railroads, the Chinese question was not ignored. In May the "People's Protective Alliance" was formed for the purpose of securing the united action of all working people in the state. Chapters were formed in San Francisco, Sacramento, Santa Clara, and Alameda counties. In November the Alliance held a largely attended convention, demanding the abrogation of the Burlingame Treaty and protection from "the ruinous competition of this servile and degraded people." Plans were formulated for the first petitions to Congress.[25] It was under these circumstances that the Democratic convention declared:

> That we regard the presence of the Chinese in our midst as an unmixed evil, ruinous alike to the people and the state, while the prospect of an increase of their numbers is appalling to the hearts of all; and we demand that the incoming legislature, through its own enactments and its urgent appeals to congress, take steps not merely to prevent the further influx of the mongolian horde upon us, but to secure the speedy exodus of those already here; and to this end we urge that measures be at once instituted to decrease the subsidy to the Pacific Mail Steamship Company, and to abrogate the so-called Burlingame treaty.[26]

In the election of 1875 neither the Republicans nor the Independents mentioned the Chinese, but the Democrats demanded such modification of the Burlingame Treaty as should make it merely a commercial agreement. The results of this election, however, seem to have made a very deep impression upon the Republicans. They no longer considered it safe to ignore the Chinese, and in two conventions held the following year adopted strong resolutions claiming that, while the Democrats had done much resolving on the question, the Republicans had brought about the only laws for relief, and demanding such modification of the Burlingame Treaty as would entirely prevent further immigration of the Chinese. The Independents disappeared as a separate party. The Democrats demanded the cessation of Chinese immigration, and pointed to the strong position taken by the national platform as promising certain relief for California.[27] With this election the Chinese question became very much a one-sided affair, the principal difference between the parties being in the kind and extent of the remedy to be applied.

The record of the activities of labor groups, mobs, and political parties has been carried forward to the middle of the decade of the

[24]*Alta*, May 27, 1877. *Chronicle*, March 30, April 9, 11, 1877. The policy of violence was urged on by the *Post*, Aug. 2, 9, 1877.
[25]*Alta*, May 9, June 10, Oct. 22, Nov. 12, 14, 1873; Feb. 4, 13, 1874. Two petitions were sent, totaling more than 22,000 names.
[26]Davis, *Political Conventions*, 327. The Independent Party made similar demands, while the Republicans issued no platform.
[27]Davis, *Political Conventions*, 339-352 (1875), 356-365 (1876).

'seventies in order to show the character of the propaganda with which the movement was promoted. We have now to indicate the legislative actions which were the inevitable outcome of this agitation. Attention already has been directed to the question of citizenship which, by 1870, had been rather definitely settled by the Federal government. A question of similar character was that of the relation of Chinese to the public schools. During the early years it was not a matter of importance, for there were very few Chinese children in California. But as their number increased they began to attract attention. A law passed in 1860 required that Negroes, Mongolians, and Indians be excluded from the public schools, and authorized the superintendent of public instruction to with-hold state funds from any school which permitted these groups to attend. Officials were permitted to furnish separate schools for them at public expense and, if the parents or guardians of ten or more children of these groups made written application, the officials were required to establish a separate school for them. In the revised law of 1866 school officials were authorized, in case these colored children could not be cared for in any other way, to permit them to attend with white children, provided the majority of the parents of the white children did not make objection in writing.[28]

In 1870 all legislation affecting the public schools was reorganized into one act, called the "California School Law," repealing everything not included in this act. The Chinese were not mentioned, and in two instances the wording indicates that the omission was intentional. One section required that "Every school, unless otherwise provided by special law, shall be open for the admission of all white children, between five and twenty-one years of age. . . . . " The other provided that "The education of children of African descent, and Indian children, shall be provided for in separate schools." In spite of several petitions from ministers and Chinese this act remained the law, so far as the Chinese were concerned, throughout the following decade. Not until 1880 was every school required to admit all children between six and seventeen years of age. When the courts ruled that a board of education could not exclude the Chinese solely on account of race the law was amended to permit separate schools for Chinese children.[29]

The most radical legislation against the Chinese during this period was to be found in municipal ordinances, especially those of San Francisco, where more than one-half of all Chinese in the state were located.

---

[28]Cal. Statutes, 1860, 325; 1863, 210; 1863-64, 213; 1865-66, 398. San Francisco Municipal Reports, 1859-60, 64, 67-68. An increasingly large number of the older Chinese boys were receiving instruction in English through several of the churches.
[29]Cal. Statutes, 1869-70, 838, 839; 1885, 100. Acts Amendatory to the Codes of California, 1880, 38. Tape v. Hurley, 5 West Coast Reporter, 692. Bulletin, Aug. 22, 1877, July 8, 1882. Call, March 7, 1878.

Here an ever-present source of inspiration for anti-Chinese sentiment was found in Chinatown. Increased immigration had produced greater congestion than ever before, and brought from the city health officer this report:

Notwithstanding politicians and demagogues have mounted this hobby for the purpose of bringing themselves into public favor, there is no disguising the fact, that they are not only a moral leper in our community, but their habits and manner of life are of such a character as to breed and engender disease wherever they reside. . . . . Dwelling as they do in the very center of the city, any contagious disease would necessarily spread with frightful rapidity. . . . . As a class, their mode of life is the most abject in which it is possible for human beings to exist. The great majority of them live crowded together in rickety, filthy and dilapidated tenement houses, like so many cattle and hogs. Considering their mode of life, it is indeed wonderful that they have so far escaped every phase of disease. In passing through that portion of the city occupied by them, the most absolute squalidness and misery meets one at every turn. Vice in all its hideousness is on every hand. Apartments that would be deemed small for the accommodation of a single American, are occupied by six, eight, or ten Mongolians, with seeming indifference to all comforts. Nothing short of ocular demonstration can convey an idea, of Chinese poverty and depravity.[30]

This report was made during the same summer in which labor groups and the unemployed were holding meetings and conducting their first great parade. Following an investigation, made at the behest of the Anti-Coolie Association, and largely to quiet the first high tide of anti-coolie sentiment, the Board of Supervisors enacted the Lodging House Ordinance, commonly called the "Cubic Air" Ordinance, from the fact that it required every lodging house to provide at least five hundred cubic feet of air space for each lodger. For violators, whether landlord or lodger, the penalty was fixed at from ten to five hundred dollars fine or imprisonment for from five to ninety days.[31] But as in the case of much of the anti-Chinese legislation, this ordinance was not enforced with any degree of consistency. Three years later it was said, "The ordinance is utterly disregarded in the Chinese quarters," and a new drive was launched. Fifty-one men were fined ten dollars each in one day, bringing consternation to Chinatown. The next day another group received like sentences, but refused to pay the fines, filling the jail to more than normal capacity. In this dilemma the Board of Supervisors passed the famous "Queue Ordinance," with the drastic requirement that every male prisoner sentenced to jail should have his hair cut to within one inch of his scalp. Mayor Alvord vetoed this ordinance on the ground that it violated the city charter, the Burlingame Treaty, and the Civil Rights Act. The veto was sustained and won strong approval, not only from the leading San Francisco newspapers, but from those of the state and in the east. Partly

---

[30]*Municipal Reports, 1869-70*, 233.
[31]*Municipal Reports, 1871-72*, 592. *Bulletin,* June 14, July 19, 26, 1870.

because of the difficulty in housing the prisoners, and partly because of an adverse decision in a local court, the "Cubic Air" Ordinance was not enforced during the next three years.[32]

Accompanying the "Queue Ordinance" was another piece of local legislation, requiring every laundry employing one horse-drawn vehicle to pay two dollars a quarter license fee, those employing two such vehicles four dollars a quarter, and those using none, fifteen dollars a quarter. Since practically all of the Chinese laundries came under the third classification the discriminatory character of the ordinance is obvious. Mayor Alvord vetoed this measure also. After some delay the veto was overridden, but the ordinance was not enforced for a year, and then the county court declared it unconstitutional.[33]

Chinese women afforded an ever-available point of attack. The state legislation of 1855 was held to be an invasion of the exclusive power of Congress to regulate commerce, but since most of the Chinese women were popularly believed to come for immoral purposes, it was felt that their regulation should come within the police power. As early as 1860 the police of San Francisco had asked for a special committee to investigate Chinese prostitution, and in 1865 they were authorized to remove Chinese public houses to parts of the city where they would be less offensive to public opinion. A few months later the legislature enacted a law declaring all such houses, "kept, managed, inhabited, or used by Chinese women for the purposes of common prostitution," to be public nuisances, common repute to be accepted as competent evidence. Leases were declared invalid, and landlords were made liable to heavy fines.[34]

With the intensified feeling of the later 'sixties, however, it was felt that these measures were inadequate. In 1870 the legislature passed a new act to deal with this problem. It was made unlawful to land any Mongolian, Chinese, or Japanese female, without first presenting satisfactory evidence that her coming was voluntary and that she was a person of correct habits and good character. Fines of from one to five thousand dollars, or imprisonment for from two to twelve months, or both fine and imprisonment, were prescribed, and each person so landed was to constitute a separate offense. At the same time these regulations were extended to Chinese males.[35]

These acts were never enforced, due to the passage of the Civil Rights Act. But four years later a similar act was passed. The Commissioner of

---

[32]*Bulletin*, May 20-22, 27, June 2, 3, 10, 24, Sept. 9, 1873. *Alta*, May 27, June 3, 24, 25, 1873. The idea of having the Chinese accept a jail sentence instead of paying the fine was undoubtedly suggested by Frederick A. Bee, attorney for the Chinese.

[33]*Municipal Reports, 1871-72*, 550. Gibson, *Chinese in America*, 282-284. *Bulletin*, June 3, 10, 24, July 1, 8, 1873.

[34]*Cal. Statutes, 1865-66*, 641-642. *Municipal Reports, 1859-60*, 62-63; *1865-66*, 124-126.

[35]*Cal. Statutes, 1869-70*, 330-333.

Immigration was required to satisfy himself as to whether any passengers on incoming ships, who were not citizens of the United States, were lunatic, idiotic, or likely to become a public charge, or a criminal, or "a lewd or debauched woman." For each such person the owner, master, or consignee of the ship must post a bond of five hundred dollars in United States gold coin against that passenger's becoming a charge to any city for two years, or convey the passenger from the state. The bond might be commuted into cash, in such amount as the Commissioner might name, of which amount he was entitled to retain twenty per cent.[36] This law immediately came before the courts. Habeas corpus proceedings were taken through the district and state supreme courts, which upheld the law. The United States Circuit and Supreme Courts, however, declared the law unconstitutional, on the grounds that it exceeded the police power of the state and violated the Burlingame Treaty, the Fourteenth Amendment, and the Civil Rights Act. The Supreme Court used very sarcastic language in characterizing the measure:

It is a most extraordinary statute. . . . . It is hardly possible to conceive a statute more skilfully framed, to place in the hands of a single man the power to prevent entirely vessels engaged in a foreign trade, say with China, from carrying passengers, or to compel them to submit to systematic extortion of the grossest kind.[37]

Shortly before the enactment of this law the city of San Francisco passed an ordinance to deal with the same problem. This ordinance made it unlawful to sell or attempt to sell any human being; to claim the services or possession of any human being, or to persuade any person to be in a condition of servitude, except as authorized by law; to enter or dwell in a brothel; to demand or receive any person or thing for any claim to the possession or services of any human being who had been bought, sold, or held in violation of this ordinance; or to threaten any person for assisting any person claimed or held in violation of this ordinance. That this legislation was directed against the traffic in Chinese women is quite apparent, but it is made even more obvious by the wording of another paragraph, which declared it unlawful,

On account of any real or pretended debt due, or pretended to be due, by any person, or any passage money paid for, or money advanced to any person, whether in this state or elsewhere, to hold or attempt to hold the person, or claim the services or possession of any human being, except in cases authorized by law.

In fact, this paragraph is almost a description of the methods used by

---

[36] *Acts Amendatory to the Codes, 1873-74,* 39.
[37] 92 U. S., 275 f. While the Chinese women were represented by the Attorney General of the United States, California submitted no defense of the statute. See also 3 Sawyer, 144. *Alta,* Aug. 24, 26, 27, 29, Sept. 14, 22, 28, 1874. Gibson, *Chinese in America,* 140-157. It was this decision which convinced anti-Chinese leaders that they must rely upon Congress for relief, and precipitated the California senate investigation and, indirectly the Congressional investigation, in 1876. *Bulletin,* March 21, 1876; Sacramento *Bee,* April 5, 1876.

procurers engaged in this traffic on the coast, as told by both the friends and the opponents of the Chinese.[38]

The Chinese were accused of introducing foreign diseases into California. Having just experienced an epidemic of smallpox, the San Francisco Board of Supervisors in 1870 enacted that the Health Officer should board every ship which brought passengers from Asiatic ports, "and then and there . . . . vaccinate each and every one of said passengers before they shall be permitted to land in the City and County of San Francisco." Two years later free vaccination was provided and strict regulations adopted for the reporting and isolation of cases and the fumigation of premises. In spite of these precautions another epidemic appeared in 1876, concerning the source of which the Health Officer was quite positive:

> I unhesitatingly declare my belief that this cause is the presence in our midst of 30,000 (as a class) of unscrupulous, lying, and treacherous Chinamen, who have disregarded our sanitary laws, concealed and are concealing their cases of smallpox, which are only known to exist by the certificates of their deaths furnished by the City Physician, unless by accident some living case is discovered. Worse than this, as a rule, their dead bodies are removed to some obscure place from the residence in which they died, so that it is impossible to disinfect their houses, for by no ingenuity can it be discovered whence the dead bodies have been removed. . . . . That this laboratory of infection—situated in the very heart of our city, distilling its poison by day and by night, and sending it forth to contaminate the atmosphere of the streets and houses of a populous, wealthy and intelligent community—is permitted to exist, is a disgrace to the civilization of the age.[39]

While this report bears evidence of being a political document there was reason for concern, with almost five hundred deaths from smallpox in thirteen months. These conditions probably were the basis of Mayor Bryant's recommendation that Hong Kong be declared an infected port, and that all vessels from that port with passengers be quarantined for thirty days before unloading. Strangely enough, the Board of Supervisors did not act upon this suggestion.

One other health regulation which applied particularly to the Chinese was distinctive, if for no other reason than that it won approval in the Federal courts. Many Californians looked upon the custom of disinterring the bodies of deceased Chinese for the purpose of sending them back to China as an expression of superstition and of contempt for America and, in addition, accused the Chinese of littering up the cemeteries with debris. With a view to reducing this practice to a minimum the legislature prohibited the removal of a body from the county in which it was buried without a permit from the local health officer. In order to

---

[38]*Municipal Reports, 1874-75*, 812-813. Reenacted in 1880. *General Orders, 1888*, 34-35. See Gibson, *Chinese in America*, 127-157; *Report 689*, 145-150, 194-195.
[39]*Municipal Reports, 1871-72*, 563-566, 606-611. Reenacted in 1880. *General Orders, 1888*, 110-115. *Municipal Reports, 1876-77*, 397. *Chronicle*, Dec. 17, 1878.

secure this permit a statement must be presented, signed by the coroner or by a reputable physician, setting forth the cause of death, and the remains must be sealed in a metal casket. The United States Circuit Court held that this act came within the police power of the state, and that it did not violate the constitution in regard to the regulation of commerce, nor was it in conflict with either the Fourteenth Amendment or the Burlingame Treaty.[40]

It would be impossible to present all of the state and municipal legislation enacted against the Chinese during this period. But in addition to the more or less outstanding measures, several of minor import, but indicating the prevailing attitude, may be noted. In order to prevent Chinese theatres from running until the early morning hours the San Francisco authorities passed an ordinance forbidding anyone to participate in or to attend any theatrical performance between the hours of one and six in the morning, or to disturb the peace by making any unusual noise in connection with any theatrical performance. The state legislature, in appropriating five hundred dollars a month for the support of the California Labor and Employment Exchange, added the stipulation, "The above appropriation is made upon the express condition that the benefits of the said Exchange shall be open and free to all persons, except Mongolians." In case this provision were violated the appropriation was to be withheld. And in creating the West Side Irrigation District, the use of Chinese labor on ditches and canals was specifically prohibited.[41]

In this chapter an attempt has been made to show how state and local authorities, in response to the agitation by organized labor and anti-coolie clubs, and to meet the exigencies of politics, sought to deal with the problems arising from the presence of the Chinese in California, prior to the meeting of the second constitutional convention. It can hardly be said that there was any coherent philosophy or program underlying these enactments; rather, a spirit of opportunism is evident throughout this period. As need arose laws were enforced, or reinforced with new ones, with periods of seeming indifference between occasions. At first the effort was to keep the Chinese out of the mines. By a rather fantastic court decision they were prevented from testifying in the courts, and then they were kept from citizenship. Throughout the period repeated efforts were made to discourage or to prevent their coming. In the later years, increased immigration and a tendency to concentrate in the cities caused the emphasis to be placed upon crowded and unsanitary living

---

[40]*Cal. Statutes, 1877-78*, 1050-1051. 6 Sawyer, 442. *Post*, May 23, 1879. At least two years must elapse between burial and removal, and a reward was offered for information regarding violators.
[41]*Municipal Reports, 1871-72*, 588. *Cal. Statutes, 1869-70*, 543; *Ibid., 1875-76*, 747.

conditions and the competition with organized labor. The influence of the latter factor became increasingly noticeable, due to the narrow margin separating the great political parties. One other element which must not be ignored is the fact that most of the measures enacted during these years were declared unconstitutional by the courts of the United States.[42]

[42]Californians watched very closely the efforts of Canada, Australia, and New Zealand in dealing with the problem of Chinese immigration. *Call,* March 20, 23, June 15, July 1, Sept. 18, 1878. *Chronicle,* Oct. 15, Nov. 18, 1878. *Bulletin,* Sept. 27, Oct. 14, Nov. 4, 18, 1878. *Post,* Sept. 30, 1878, Jan. 3, 8, May 7, 1879. Sacramento *Record-Union,* Sept. 30, 1878.

Chapter IV

THE NEW CONSTITUTION AND THE CHINESE

In a very real sense the year 1876 marked a crisis in the anti-Chinese agitation in California. Several factors accounted for this. During each of the preceding three years a greater number of Chinese had passed through the Customs House than at any time since 1852. Almost without exception the state and municipal legislation enacted for the control of this immigration had become ineffective, either because of conflict with the Burlingame Treaty, the Fourteenth Amendment, or the Civil Rights Act, or because its enforcement had proved impracticable.

At the same time the movement against the Chinese had become state-wide. The labor vote had attained such proportions in numbers and solidarity as to make election to public office almost impossible without its support, and it was generally understood that in order to secure the labor vote a candidate must declare against the Chinese.[1] In the spring of 1876 the numerous anti-Chinese clubs combined under the name of the Anti-Chinese Union, with the purpose "to unite, centralize and direct the anti-Chinese strength of our Country." Each member of a club was to be pledged to four things: to the constitution of the club, not to employ Chinese, not to purchase goods from the employer of Chinese, and not to sustain the Chinese or the employer of Chinese. The Union carried on its list of vice presidents the United States senators, congressmen, and most of the other prominent politicians of the state. It is apparent that the anti-Chinese clubs had become something more than merely labor groups.[2]

Due to existing conditions and to the experiences with local and state legislation, the leaders of the opposition to the Chinese were coming more and more to the conviction that their only hope lay in action by the Federal government. Serious obstacles, however, had to be met in this course of procedure. The question of Chinese immigration was a local problem of a section of the country which heretofore had had relatively little influence in national affairs. Furthermore, the proposals of California and the other Pacific coast states would endanger the trade and missionary activities in China, which were the chief interests of the region east of the Rockies so far as that country was concerned. Governor Bradley of Nevada was quoted as saying that the problem had been taken from the state and placed in the hands of a government three thousand

---

[1] This is evident from party platforms. Davis, *Political Conventions*, 299-300, 307-308, 334. Eaves, *California Labor Legislation*, 147.

[2] *Constitution and By-Laws of the Anti-Chinese Union of San Francisco.* A more radical organization may be seen in the *Constitution and By-Laws of the United Brothers of California*, organized the same year.

miles away, "that know as little of our wants and are as indifferent to their correction as was the Parliament under George III to the wants of the colonies a century ago."[3]

Restrictionists recognized the difficulties in securing Federal action, but they realized, also, that the national political situation was in their favor. For the first time in almost two decades the Democrats were in control of the House of Representatives, and a presidential election was at hand.

> But if it is to be attempted the session of Congress preceding a Presidential election is the most promising. The Democratic House, if a show of unanimity and determination can be presented, will not be disposed to throw away the votes of the Pacific States. . . . . The Republican Senate will be likely to be swayed by precisely the same motive. But there is work to be done of an earnest kind before any results can be reached.
>
> That failing, the working people of the Pacific Coast will be sooner or later driven to the redress of their own wrongs and the forcible removal of the vermin who are eating out their life.[4]

In the editorial discussion of succeeding months this factor was frequently stressed. The Democrats blamed the Republicans for the Burlingame Treaty and expressed despair of getting any relief from "Grant and Company," while the Republicans accused their opponents of being the first to saddle the Chinese on the country and of wanting, even yet, to use their labor in the south. It is difficult at times to determine whether a writer was concerned more with the problem of Chinese immigration or with the success of his party. The political aspects of this question need constantly to be kept in mind. Their importance during the subsequent quarter of a century may be seen in the shifting of control in Congress and in the presidency, and in the fact that, with one exception, all laws and treaties restricting Chinese immigration were enacted on the eve of national elections.

The whole question was forcibly precipitated on public attention when Mayor Bryant informed the San Francisco Board of Supervisors that the Supreme Court had declared unconstitutional the California law for the exclusion of Chinese women. Mayor Bryant's statement contained a summary of the evils of Chinese immigration, and suggested the naming of a committee of twelve prominent citizens who should decide what was to be done. He suggested, also, that a great mass meeting be held to secure the public opinion, and that a committee be sent to Washington to urge appropriate legislation. His proposals were unanimously endorsed by the Board of Supervisors. To the committee the mayor elaborated his plan and pointed out the opportune circumstances.

---

[3] *Post,* Jan. 6, 1877. See also Sacramento *Bee,* April 5, 1876.
[4] The first is from the *Bulletin,* March 23, 1876; the other from the Oakland *Transcript,* March 19, 1876. See also *Alta,* July 9, 1876; Sonoma *Democrat,* March 25, 1876.

I believe that this is the best time to go to Washington. The House is controlled by one party and the Senate by another. We are on the eve of a presidential
election and both parties are looking toward this coast for aid. If you can get a
bill before one House and have it passed, the other will not be likely to kill it.[5]

The mass meeting, which was held about two weeks later, was indeed
a notable gathering. Governor Irwin, the chairman, sounded the keynote:

It is not, then, fellow-citizens, a question merely of morals, of social conditions,
of political economy. It is all these; it is everything that goes to make up American
civilization. . . . . The subversion of our civilization is involved in this Chinese
emigration, because, if the influx of this race continues, they become the laborers
of our country. . . . . I hold, whoever would degrade the white laboring man to a
lower level than that he now holds, is an enemy of his race.

The Committee of Twelve presented a lengthy set of resolutions, labeled
"An Address to the People of California in Mass Meeting Assembled,"
but which was really an appeal to the entire nation on behalf of California
against the Chinese, setting forth in strong and vivid language the evils
under which the state was suffering. These resolutions were endorsed
by the meeting "with great acclaim." Similar meetings had been held in
other cities and delegates sent to the San Francisco gathering. Later a
committee of three was appointed to present California's grievances to
Congress and to President Grant.[6]

It may readily be seen that this mass meeting, while emphasizing the
interests of labor, was not under the leadership primarily of labor groups.
The outstanding political leaders of the state were conspicuous here as in
the Anti-Chinese Union. Several reasons may account for this. Some
were undoubtedly influenced by hope of political advancement. Others
may have been impelled by a desire to have a troublesome problem
settled, while still others were unquestionably influenced by the dangers
which lay in permitting the movement to get out of control. That feeling
was very intense, and that some were fearful of rioting is evident from
a series of editorials by Henry C. Beals in the *Commercial Herald and
Market Review*.[7] This is borne out by the actions of the Chinese. The
heads of the Six Companies and the Chinese Merchants' Exchange cabled
officials in China to prevent the coming of immigrants, because of the
danger to life and property. They also wrote a letter to the mayor and to
the chief of police asking for protection, and published an address to the
American public, asking that any move for the restriction of their coming
be accomplished by peaceful methods.[8]

[5]*Alta*, March 23, 1876. *Bulletin*, March 21, 23, 1876.
[6]*Chronicle*, April 6, 1876. *Alta*, April 6, May 9, 1876. Stockton *Independent*, May 18, 1876.
Sacramento *Bee*, April 4, 1876. F. M. Pixley, P. A. Roach, and M. L. McDonald composed the
committee, and may have helped in securing the appointment of the Joint Special Committee of
Congress.
[7]Issues of March 30, April 6, 13, 27, May 11, 25, June 29, 1876. Reprinted in *Report 689*,
1184-1189.
[8]*Alta*, March 30, April 4, 5, 1876. *Chronicle*, April 1, 6, 1876. The *Alta* stated that this
affair led the Chinese to ask for a consul at San Francisco. See also Gibson, *Chinese in America*,
300-324.

What may be termed an epilogue to this agitation occurred the following November, when the Joint Special Committee of Congress was in
San Francisco. A great torchlight parade was staged by labor organizations and anti-coolie clubs. That it was intended to influence the committee is evident from the transparencies carried through the streets,
bearing such slogans as "We will not give up our country to the Chinese,"
"Our rights we will maintain," "We denounce the evidence of Chinese
hirelings," and "White labor must triumph."[9] There was evident in both
of these meetings the purpose of the more conservative people of the
community to bring all possible pressure to bear upon the national government to restrict Chinese immigration, and to curb all violence, because
they realized that this feature stirred the sympathies of the east in favor
of the Chinese. This marks a new phase in the anti-Chinese movement.

The great task before the anti-Chinese forces of California was to
convince the rest of the country of the need for excluding the Chinese.
This purpose of "education" was back of the great April mass meetings
and of the delegation to Washington. But of much greater significance
was the action of the state senate in appointing a special investigating
committee to inquire,

1. As to the number of Chinese in this state, and the effect their presence has
upon the social and political condition of the state.
2. As to the probable result of Chinese immigration upon the country, if such
immigration be not discouraged.
3. As to the means of exclusion, if such committee should be of the opinion
that the presence of the Chinese element in our midst is detrimental to the interests
of the country.
4. As to such other matters as, in the judgment of the committee, have a bearing upon the question of Chinese immigration.

The committee was directed to prepare a memorial to Congress, and to
publish a sufficient number of copies of this memorial and of the testimony
to supply all of the leading newspapers of the country, besides five copies
for each member of Congress, ten for the governor of each state, and ten
thousand for general distribution.[10]

The committee was composed of five Democrats and two Republicans,
four of the number being from San Francisco and one from Sacramento,
cities with the most numerous Chinese populations and the strongest
anti-Chinese feeling in the state. If the instructions and personnel of the
committee and the state of public opinion at the time be considered, it
was hardly to be expected that an impartial inquiry would result. On the
day following the committee's authorization the *Post* declared that if the
committee would do its work thoroughly it would be able to collect in one
month evidence sufficient to convince Congress that the Chinese immi-

[9]*Bulletin,* Nov. 16, 1876. *Alta,* Nov. 16, 1876.
[10]Cal. Senate, *Chinese Immigration,* 68. The authorization was rushed through on the last
day of the session, and two days before the great meeting at San Francisco.

grants were coolies owned by the Six Companies, that this system was worse than southern slavery, and that those in this country were but the vanguard of tens of millions more who would come in the next fifty years.

With such a showing as this, presented in dignified and respectful language and backed up by facts and conclusive evidence, as it can be, there is no reason to doubt that the objects of the movement will be gained.

Altogether sixty witnesses appeared before the committee during its fifteen sessions, of whom eighteen were Chinese, including the presidents of the Six Companies. Possibly because of fear, or because they thought their efforts would be futile, or because they wished to evade giving information, the testimony of the Chinese threw very little light upon the situation, the most common answer being, "I don't know."[11] Of the forty-two white witnesses ten were members of local police forces, twelve held political office, and three had had experience in diplomatic or consular service. Of the others, four were clergymen, two manufacturers, two newspapermen, two English ship's officers, a marble worker, a lawyer, a baker, a farmer, an expressman, and two men whose occupations were not given. Nine had either lived or travelled in China. Representatives of the large transportation companies, of those interested in the China trade, and of the great landowners were conspicuous by their absence.

To attempt a detailed analysis of the mass of testimony given in this investigation would be to go beyond the scope of this chapter. But because this undertaking bulked large in the movement at the time it will be necessary to note the pronouncements of the committee to the rest of the country. In the memorial to Congress the committee declared that the one hundred and twenty-five thousand Chinese in the state were from the lowest orders, "the dregs of the population;" that included in these thousands was a large criminal class; that the Chinese had little respect for American laws, but were regulated by secret tribunals, which constituted an *imperium in imperio;* that practically all women immigrants were devoted to prostitution; that the men who were not criminals subjected American labor to a painful competition amounting in many cases to monopoly; that the bulk of this labor was servile, being imported under contract; that efforts at christianizing them had practically failed, and that there was very little hope for the future, since there were but few children to serve as the basis of progress; that the Chinese were incapable of adapting themselves to American ideas and institutions; and that the only benefit from the Chinese was "cheap labor" which, in another

---

[11]Cal. Senate, *Chinese Immigration,* 129-140, 159-176, 185-187, 198-207, 214-215. The statement of Mrs. Coolidge, that the presidents of the Six Companies refused to tell very much because they had been insulted, probably over-emphasizes the sensitiveness and underrates the shrewdness of these men in withholding information which might be used against them. *Chinese Immigration,* 87.

quarter of a century, might result in the displacement of white labor, or worse, in riot and insurrection. Three measures for relief were recommended: cooperation with Great Britain to secure the complete prohibition of the traffic in men and women; through frank negotiation to secure the abrogation of all treaties allowing the immigration of Chinese to the United States; and for immediate relief, legislation by Congress to limit this immigration to ten on any one vessel.[12]

Apparently the committee was not content with sending a memorial to Congress. It proceeded to draw up "An Address to the People of the United States upon the Evils of Chinese Immigration." The evils enumerated are very much the same as those in the memorial, but in greater detail, and the statement of each is accompanied by extensive excerpts from the testimony, as well as material not found in the record. It is not a misrepresentation to say that the "Address" is a restatement of the testimony in abbreviated form, intended for popular consumption, each main topic being prefaced with a short introductory statement, and the whole closed with a brief summary and appeal. Many people would read the "Address" who would not undertake the complete record of testimony, and for propaganda purposes it probably would be more effective.[13]

That the committee wished to make the best possible impression upon the east is evident from certain omissions of evidence. Several statements were made which furnished conclusive proof that the special police serving in the San Francisco Chinatown were in collusion with the owners of Chinese places of gambling and prostitution, since they received a large portion of their pay from these owners. This evidence was deleted from the record and published in another state document which would be read by very few people. As a result, however, of this evidence the next session of the legislature enacted that "No special police officer shall ever be appointed in that portion of said city and county known as the Chinese quarter."[14] With a similar purpose in view the legislature ordered an election to be held at which the people of California might vote for or against the coming of the Chinese. This election, held in September, 1879, resulted in less than nine hundred votes for the Chinese and more than one hundred and fifty thousand against their coming. Governor Irwin declared that this vote should be accepted as a true expression of California's opinion of the Chinese. Friends of the Chinese, however, insisted that it was not a fair vote, since only "Against Chinese Immigra-

---

[12]Cal. Senate, *Chinese Immigration*, 59-65. Mrs. Coolidge says that the first recommendation "displayed astonishing ignorance," since this trade had been forbidden by all great powers. *Chinese Immigration*, 94. But British investigations in 1876, 1877, and 1890 indicate that the practice did not end with official proclamations. Campbell, *Chinese Coolie Emigration*, 2.
[13]Cal. Senate, *Chinese Immigration*, 7-56.
[14]*Appendix to the Journals of the Senate and the Assembly, 1877-78*, III. So far as the writer has been able to discover this document of eleven pages has not been referred to in any other publication. For the new law see *Cal. Statutes, 1877-78*, 880.

tion" had been printed on the ballot, and in order to vote in their favor one must erase "Against" and write in "For."[15]

It is indicative of the intensity of feeling at this time that while political leaders were making a concerted effort to secure national action, other forces opposed to the Chinese continued to utilize local measures. The legislature which authorized the state investigating committee also enacted the "Lodging House Law," similar to the "cubic air" ordinance of San Francisco:

> Every person who owns, leases, lets, or hires, to any person or persons, any room or apartment in any building, house or other structure, within the limits of any incorporated city, or city and county, within the State of California, for the purpose of a lodging or sleeping apartment, which room or apartment contains less than five hundred cubic feet of space, in the clear, for each person so occupying such room or apartment, shall be deemed guilty of a misdemeanor, and shall, upon conviction thereof, be punished by a fine of not less than fifty (50) dollars or more than five hundred (500) dollars, or by imprisonment in the County Jail, or by both such fine and imprisonment.

Anyone occupying such a room was liable to a fine of from ten to fifty dollars or to imprisonment. Hospitals, jails, and other public institutions were excepted from the operation of this law.[16]

This legislation revived the enforcement of the "cubic air" ordinance in San Francisco. But again the officials were faced with the problem of an overcrowded jail. The old "Queue Ordinance" also was revived, in an effort to induce the Chinese to pay fines, for they seemed not to care about a five days' jail sentence. For a time this ordinance was enforced, almost solely against the Chinese, but in 1878 the United States Circuit Court held it unconstitutional. This decision made the enforcement of the "cubic air" ordinance, as well as the state law, almost impossible.[17]

No phase of the anti-Chinese agitation attracted such wide attention as the organization and brief career of the Workingmen's Party of California, under the leadership of Denis Kearney. In fact, this organization's activities were so spectacular that there has been a widespread tendency to look upon it as constituting the major part of the movement against the Chinese. The fallacy of this view should be obvious.[18]

A combination of forces brought about the organization of a separate labor party. The general depression prevailing for several years in the east reached California, accentuated by a serious drouth, a large decrease in mining returns, and a ruinous crash in stocks, whose speculations had

[15]*Cal. Statutes, 1877-78*, 3. *Appendix to the Journals of the Senate and the Assembly, 1880,* Part 5, Docs. 19, 20. *Alta,* March 28, 1878. (Augustus Layres), *The Other Side of the Chinese Question,* 15. Also a broadside, "The Pro-Chinese Minority to the American People, President, and Congress." Dec. 26 1879.
[16]*Cal. Statutes, 1875-76,* 759. Its constitutionality was upheld. See *Chronicle, Call, Bulletin,* and *Post,* April 16, 1878. One editor, protesting the discrimination in the enforcement of this law asked, "What better right has a Chinaman than a white man to be ventilated?" Sacramento *Record-Union,* Nov. 16, 1876.
[17]*Ho Ah Kow v. Matthew Nunan,* 5 Sawyer, 552-566. *Chronicle,* March 17, 1879. *Bulletin,* March 17, 1879, Dec. 21, 1881.
[18]James Bryce, *American Commonwealth* (1891), II, 385-408, 747-750.

lured great numbers of laboring men. The unemployed flocked to San Francisco, there to meet the competition of increasing numbers of Chinese. The eight-hour law secured after the election of 1867 had become practically a dead letter. The older parties frequently had expressed opposition to the coming of the Chinese, but little had been accomplished and the labor groups were becoming skeptical. By including the railroads and monopolists in general among their objects of attack they won the adherence of the Grangers and other discontented groups, and for a few years the Workingmen's Party was the anti-Chinese party *par excellence*.[19] The party had its inception in a reaction to the alarming series of railroad strikes in the east during the summer of 1877. On July 23 some six thousand workingmen of San Francisco held a meeting to express sympathy with the eastern strikers. Resolutions were adopted in which crookedness, grafting, extravagance, watered stocks, subsidies, and reduction of wages were declared to be but parts of a conspiracy for the destruction of the Republic. In spite of efforts by the chairman to prevent it, anti-coolie sentiment was injected into the meeting, while the hoodlum element rushed into Chinatown, burned several buildings, sacked fifteen washhouses, and broke windows in the Methodist Chinese Mission.[20]

These destructive activities were continued the following day, and committees of safety were organized in both Oakland and San Francisco, the latter enrolling almost seven thousand men in its "pick handle brigade," under William T. Coleman of vigilante fame. The naval authorities at Mare Island sent all available forces, and within forty-eight hours order was restored.[21] This disturbance must be kept in mind as part of the background of the Workingmen's Party, which was not a sudden movement on the part of the labor groups, but rather one for which their activities during preceding years had prepared them.

> It was a protest against the business and political corruption of the times, an effort to find relief for economic distress, an expression of class feeling that had been voiced in the bitter and extravagant oratory of the sandlot, and given literary form and extended influence by the newspapers; the whole movement being greatly assisted at every stage of its development by the folly of the San Francisco municipal authorities.[22]

In September the municipal election took place and the labor groups participated, not as a political party but as clubs. After the election these organizations did not dissolve, as had previously been the case, but instead formed a political party. Numerous meetings were held, and on October

---

[19]Eaves, *California Labor Legislation*, 27-28, 212.
[20]*Bulletin*, July 19, 20, 23-25, 1877.
[21]*Bulletin*, July 25-28, 30, 31, 1877. Williams, *San Francisco Committee of Vigilance*, 407-408. Denis Kearney was a member of the San Francisco committee, and according to Henry George, learned from this how to run his party. "The Kearney Agitation in California," *Popular Science Monthly*, vol. 17, pp. 433 ff., August, 1880.
[22]Eaves, *California Labor Legislation*, 20-21, 28-29, 38-39.

5 Denis Kearney was elected president, J. G. Day vice president, and H. L. Knight secretary. A set of principles was adopted, declaring it to be the object of the new party to unite all of the poor and laboring men into one group for defense against the encroachment of capital. They proposed to take the government out of the hands of the rich and place it in those of the people, to rid the country of cheap Chinese labor, to destroy land monopoly and the money power of the rich, to provide for the poor and unfortunate, to elect none but workingmen and their friends to office, and to secure the discharge of all Chinese employed in the state. While the party would not encourage riot or outrage, neither would it volunteer to suppress those who became impatient. "Let those who raise the storm by their selfishness, suppress it themselves. If they dare raise the devil, let them meet him face to face. We will not help them."[23]

It is apparent that Chinese labor was not the only problem confronting California workingmen. In later resolutions many other items were included, such as the direct election of the president, the eight-hour day, life imprisonment for malfeasance in office, abolition of prison contract labor, compulsory education for all children, the single tax for farm lands, abolition of punishment by fine, of the executive pardoning power, and of the fee system for paying public officials. But opposition to Chinese immigration appeared in every set of resolutions, in some form of the following:

The Chinese laborer is a curse to our land, is degrading to our morals, is a menace to our liberties, and should be restricted and forever abolished, and "the Chinese must go."[24]

Chinese labor provided the emotional drive and concrete motivation necessary for uniting the workingmen of the state. Their exclusion constituted at least one means to the desired end. This was most forcibly expressed in Kearney's "Manifesto."

We have made no secret of our intentions. We make none. Before you and before the world we declare that the Chinaman must leave our shores. We declare that white men, and women, and boys, and girls, cannot live as the people of the great republic should and compete with the single Chinese coolie in the labor market. We declare that we cannot hope to drive the Chinaman away by working cheaper than he does. None but an enemy would expect it of us; none but an idiot could hope for success; none but a degraded coward and slave would make the effort. To an American, death is preferable to life on a par with the Chinaman.

The only peaceable means left was to organize and "vote the moon-eyed nuisance out of the country." If this failed, then workingmen would be justified in using force to accomplish their objective.[25]

[23]Davis, *Political Conventions*, 366-367. See also Bryce, *American Commonwealth*, II, 391-393.
[24]Davis, *Political Conventions*, 385. See pages 377-381, 383-388.
[25]*Chronicle*, Oct. 16, 1877.

During succeeding months the story of the Workingmen's Party is one of written and oral appeals, conventions, and parades. On two occasions the Chinese appealed for protection, once to the mayor of San Francisco and the other to the President of the United States. For several days Kearney and others were under arrest, but the charges were dismissed. During these months the party was making rapid progress, with branches all over the state, as far south as Los Angeles. In Oakland and in Santa Clara county Workingmen's candidates were elected to fill vacancies in the legislature. In March, Sacramento and Oakland elected complete Workingmen's tickets to fill the municipal offices. But the climax of the party's prestige was reached in June when, in spite of a fusion ticket set up by the Republicans and Democrats, the Workingmen won one-third of the total number of seats in the state constitutional convention.[26]

During the summer Kearney went east, speaking in the interest of the gubernatorial campaign of General Benjamin F. Butler in Massachusetts and attempting to organize a national workingmen's party. In San Francisco the Workingmen brought pressure on the Board of Supervisors to remove the Chinese quarter out of the city. The Board made an inspection and found ample cause for removal, but justified inaction on the ground of lack of authority.[27] When news came early in February that Congress had passed the Fifteen Passenger Bill the Workingmen and the Democrats fell to quarreling over which party should receive the major credit for this victory. The blame for the veto of this bill was laid on Kearney and his agitation, on the ground that people in the east confused the entire anti-Chinese movement with "Kearneyism." The Workingmen countered with the claim that they had done more in one year than the old parties in twenty years to bring the matter to national attention, and that the only hope of eradicating the Chinese lay in the leadership of Kearney and the Workingmen's Party.

Local and state efforts against the Chinese reached a climax in connection with the adoption of California's second constitution. The first constitution had been hastily drawn up by men whose experience in California was measured only by months. In the 'seventies numerous factors, some of which had been accumulating for years, came to a focus. Agriculture had become more important than mining, but the lure of the great "strikes" led to a frenzy of speculation in mining stocks and brought tragedy to thousands when the companies suspended dividends in Janu-

---

[26]Davis, *Political Conventions*, 371-375, 381-390. *Bulletin*, Nov. 28, 30, 1877. *Post* and *Chronicle*, Dec. 28, 1877. *Call*, Nov. 24, 1877. Halls were closed to the Workingmen, and the legislature sought to restrict liberty of speech. *Acts Amendatory to the Codes of California*, *1877-78*, 117-118. Bryce, *American Commonwealth*, II, 749.

[27]*Chronicle*, June 2, July 18, 25, Aug. 1, 10, 1878. *Bulletin*, July 21, 23, 1878. *Call*, July 24, Aug. 1, 2, 1878.

ary, 1877.[28] During this winter California experienced one of the worst drouths in its history, causing great losses to farmers and cattlemen, and closing many mines. At the same time the depression over the state became more acute, causing a great increase in the number of unemployed.

To these factors must be added others, less concrete but none the less real. The railroads were accused of charging exorbitant rates, of discriminating between communities and individuals, of controlling the state government, of unfair dealings in connection with land grants, and of failing to pay their just share of taxes. After years of unsettled conditions as to titles, most of the good land had passed under the control of large holders, who were accused of shutting out the small owner and of seeking to establish a manorial system based upon the use of Chinese labor. Since the Chinese were employed by most of the corporations, whether engaged in transportation, in manufacturing, or in land development, they were opposed not merely as competitors for employment, but also as tools of the capitalists in their efforts to control the economic and political life of the state. Thus the Chinese, who formed a concrete source of irritation, were made a definite point of attack for the solution of a situation which, of course, had its origin much deeper.[29]

Under these conditions it is not surprising that the proposal for a new constitution received the approval of a majority of the voters. Delegates were elected in June, 1878, when the Workingmen were at the peak of their enthusiasm. The conservatives, uniting on a Non-Partisan ticket, elected seventy-eight, the Workingmen fifty-one, the Democrats ten, the Republicans eleven, and the Independents two. The seeming two-to-one majority against the Workingmen did not materialize, for many of the other delegates demanded the same reforms that the Workingmen were urging, and the Non-Partisans were able, after several ballots, to elect Joseph P. Hoge as president of the convention by a majority of only one vote, and their candidate for secretary was defeated.[30]

Chinese immigration was one of the three most prominent controversial questions before the convention, the other two being corporations and taxation. Most of the conservatives held that the problem was entirely in the hands of Congress. The Workingmen's delegates and others, however, were convinced that, in spite of decisions of the Supreme Court, the state must have the power to protect itself against this evil. As a

---

[28]The two principal companies were the Consolidated Virginia and the California, the former paying $1,000,000 a month in dividends. J. S. Hittell, *History of San Francisco* (1878), 423-424. The correlation between losses in this speculation and the enmity toward capitalists has not been worked out.

[29]For illuminating discussions see Cleland, *California*, 402-422, and Carl Brent Swisher, *Motivation and Political Technique in the California Constitutional Convention, 1878-1879* (1930), Chapter I.

[30]*Debates and Proceedings of the Constitutional Convention of the State of California*, I, 11-12, 21. Davis, *Political Conventions*, 381-383, 390-392. Swisher, *California Constitutional Convention*, 18-28. *Alta*, April 11-13, 15, 18, 27, May 5, 1878.

consequence, the convention was deluged with all sorts of proposals, ranging from the laconic "Resolved, 'The Chinese Must Go,'" to one which provided in detail for such conditions as would have made it almost impossible for any Chinese to exist. In view of the situation in the state at the time we may readily agree that "No body of legislators were ever confronted with a more impossible task."[31]

In solving this dilemma the convention took hold of both horns. A memorial addressed to both houses of Congress was adopted, calling attention to the petitions which the people of California, "as became a people devoted to the National Union, and filled with profound reverence for law," had repeatedly addressed to the national government. Amazement was expressed at the long delay in responding to these petitions, and the opposition to the Chinese was declared to be so universal and strong that California, more interested in the China trade than any other part of the country, was willing to forego all benefits of that trade rather than continue to suffer from Chinese immigration. Then the memorial summarized the reasons for this opposition, stressing the danger of an immense increase due to famine in north China, the secret tribunals, the crowding, the diseases, the lack of assimilation, and the degrading effect of a quasi-slave labor system. Whatever means within the police power it might possess California proposed to use, but it very earnestly asked of Congress the enacting of "such prohibitory legislation as will effectively prevent the further immigration of Chinese coolies or laborers into the American parts of this coast." In an effort to make this appeal more effective the convention urged the governors of Oregon, Nevada, Washington, Idaho, Montana, and Arizona to have memorials sent to the national government, asking for such modification of the Burlingame Treaty as would prevent the further immigration of Chinese to the United States.[32]

As was to be expected, the attempt to write effective measures into the constitution occupied a great deal more of the convention's time than the memorial. The committee on the Chinese presented a report containing nine sections, only the first of which had the unanimous approval of the committee. This section granted to the legislature authority to provide for the protection of the state and the local communities against alien vagrants, paupers, mendicants, criminals, and persons afflicted with contagious or infectious disease, or who might in any way be dangerous to the welfare of the state, and to provide for their removal from the state in case they refused to comply with this legislation.[33]

The opening speech of the debate was made by the chairman, John F. Miller, and was considered the strongest presentation of the case for

[31]Eaves, *California Labor Legislation*, 151. *Debates*, I, 84, 92.
[32]*Debates*, I, 77, 92, 157, 627; II, 645, 677-679, 709-712, 739, 756.
[33]*Debates*, I, 248. This reference covers the entire report.

restriction in the entire discussion. He stated that this section proceeded upon the theory that the state did not have the power to prohibit immigration, but that it must deal with the Chinese as part of the state's population, under the police power. He considered this section the only part of the report that would be upheld by the Federal courts. Speaking of the competition of Chinese labor and the "brotherhood of man" argument he said,

> The Chinaman is the result of training in the art of low life. . . . . Turn out your finest thoroughbred horses to roam the plain with mustangs . . . . and see the operation of the law of the survival of the fittest. . . . . It is in the economy of Providence that man shall exist in nationalities, and that they shall be divided by the antipathies of race.

Practically the only opposition to this section was because of its leniency, but a proposed substitute requiring all mayors and boards of supervisors to see that no Chinese should be allowed to continue in their respective jurisdictions, was voted down.[34]

The second section provided that any corporation doing business in the state should lose all legal rights under its franchise if it employed foreigners ineligible to become citizens. This provoked a very spirited discussion and several amendments were offered. One which was seriously considered would have required an alien, before he could engage in any employment, to secure a "certificate of authority" which, however, should not be issued to aliens ineligible to citizenship. Employers would be subject to prosecution in case of violation. It was in this connection that a very strong plea was made for the right of the states to exclude "anything which may corrupt the morals or endanger the health or lives of their citizens." The amendment was defeated, however, and the section was adopted essentially as it came from the committee, except that "Chinese or Mongolians" were expressly mentioned. And then, having made so sweeping an application of the principle of non-employment, it was a simple matter to extend it to the public works of state, county, and municipality, which was done in section three, practically without debate.[35]

No part of the committee's report occasioned more debate than section four, which would have prohibited all further immigration of Chinese into the state. This section, the result of numerous proposals submitted to the committee, more than any other raised the question of the relation between state and federal governments in the control of commerce. The classic interpretation, of course, had been in the Passenger Cases, thirty years before this. But James J. Ayers, editor of the Los Angeles *Express*, contended that Congress did not possess the *exclusive* right to regulate commerce. For his constitutional argument he went back to the earlier case of *New York v. Miln* and also quoted the minority in the Passenger

---

[34]*Debates*, I, 633 ff.; II, 653, 668.
[35]*Debates*, II, 655-667, 699-702.

Cases. But his claim was based fundamentally upon the broad ground of the right of every community to protect itself against dangers to its peace, well-being, and prosperity, which he said the Supreme Court had never denied.

The argument of Ayers was answered by C. V. Stuart, a Sonoma county farmer, and the only man in the convention to come out boldly in defense of Chinese immigration, claiming that, instead of ruining the state, it had made the state what it was. Pointing out that Ayers had quoted principally minority opinions, he added,

> He also quoted very lengthily from Roger Taney. I remember when Taney made another decision. Do you know what became of it? I remember the Dred Scott decision, ... and I remember what that led to, and I think you do too.

After a debate lasting five days the section was eliminated, part of the evidence, as Swisher says, "of the extent to which the convention had quailed before the lash of unconstitutionality."[36]

Section five was very much like section four in its purpose, and many of the same arguments were used for and against it. But the debate was notable because of the opposition to the Chinese expressed by delegates from outside the large centers, especially the farmers. Undoubtedly the nature of the proposal accounted for this, since it involved the right of a person ineligible to citizenship to settle in the state. Henry Larkin, a prominent farmer of El Dorado county, presented what was probably the extreme expression of racial antipathy during the convention.

> This State should be a State for white men, without any respect to the treaty, or misinterpretation of any treaty. The State has the right of self-preservation. It is the same right that a man of family has to protect his house and home. . . . . We want no other race here. The future of this republic demands that it shall be a white man's government, and that all other races shall be excluded.

Others argued that since the Federal government had discriminated against the Chinese by excluding them from the privilege of homesteading, the state should have the right to exclude them from leasing or owning land. When opponents of the section urged that it violated the treaty rights of the Chinese, Ayers and others declared that if the treaty took this power from the state it was unconstitutional and void. The section, retained by the committee of the whole, was stricken out on second reading.[37]

The sixth section proposed to bar foreigners ineligible to citizenship from suing or being sued, from fishing in the waters of the state, from receiving license to carry on any occupation, and from owning or leasing any real property. In a poorly attended session the time was occupied principally in attempting to add amendments, most of the debate centering

[36]*Debates,* II, 634-704. Swisher, *California Constitutional Convention,* 91. The vote was 54 to 51.
[37]*Debates,* II, 704-713; III, 1429. The vote was 61 to 60.

about the constitutionality of the provisions. On second reading this section was strongly opposed by the more conservative members, not only as being unconstitutional, but as disgracing the state in the eyes of the east and doing more harm than good, since it would "furnish our enemies with a club with which to beat our brains out." The section was omitted.[38]

The defeat of section four increased the importance of section seven. It authorized the legislature to do all in its power to discourage the immigration into the state of foreigners ineligible to citizenship, to provide for their exclusion from the state, and to delegate all necessary power to cities for the removal of such foreigners outside their limits. By a series of amendments the exclusion clause was eliminated, and others were added prohibiting "Asiatic coolieism" and authorizing the legislature to prohibit the introduction of Chinese into the state. The debate centered principally about the existence of coolieism, and the section was accepted with less opposition than its provisions might have warranted.[39]

The last two sections of the report were much alike. The one forbade the employment of Chinese by public officers and disqualified for public office any person who, within three months before an election, employed Chinese. The other disfranchised all employers of Chinese. After very brief consideration both were stricken out on the ground of unconstitutionality.[40]

The article on the Chinese, as written into the new constitution, contained the following provisions:

Section 1. The Legislature shall prescribe all necessary regulations for the protection of the State, and the counties, cities, and towns thereof, from the burdens and evils arising from the presence of aliens, who are or may become vagrants, paupers, mendicants, criminals, or invalids afflicted with contagious or infectious diseases, and from aliens otherwise dangerous or detrimental to the well-being or peace of the State, and to impose conditions upon which such persons may reside in the State, and to provide the means and mode of their removal from the State upon failure or refusal to comply with such conditions; provided, that nothing contained in this section shall be construed to impair or limit the power of the Legislature to pass such police laws or other regulations as it may deem necessary.

Section 2. No corporation now existing or hereafter formed under the laws of this State, shall, after the adoption of this Constitution, employ, directly or indirectly, in any capacity, any Chinese or Mongolian. The Legislature shall pass such laws as may be necessary to enforce this provision.

Section 3. No Chinese shall be employed on any State, county, municipal, or other public work, except in punishment for crime.

Section 4. The presence of foreigners ineligible to become citizens of the United States is declared to be dangerous to the well-being of the State, and the

---

[38]*Debates*, II, 714-717; III, 1429-1430. The debate was enlivened by a proposal to deprive ministers and physicians of their professional privileges and citizenship if they served Chinese. The proposal was ruled out of order as frivolous.

[39]*Debates*, II, 720-727.

[40]*Debates*, II, 728-729. Miller characterized sections five to nine as "starvation by constitutional provision." *Ibid.*, I, 630.

Legislature shall discourage their immigration by all the means within its power. Asiatic coolieism is a form of human slavery, and is forever prohibited in this State; and all contracts for coolie labor shall be void. All companies or corporations, whether formed in this country or any foreign country, for the importation of such labor, shall be subject to such penalties as the Legislature may prescribe. The Legislature shall delegate all necessary power to the incorporated cities and towns of this State for the removal of Chinese without the limits of such cities and towns, or for their location within prescribed portions of those limits; and it shall also provide the necessary legislation to prohibit the introduction into this State of Chinese after the adoption of this Constitution. This section shall be enforced by appropriate legislation.

The constitution contained two other discriminations against the Chinese. By silence, natives of China were denied the right to own and inherit land.

Foreigners of the white race, or of African descent, eligible to become citizens of the United States under the naturalization laws thereof, while bona fide residents of this State, shall have the same rights in respect to the acquisition, possession, enjoyment, transmission, and inheritance of property as native-born citizens.

In this section an object which had been defeated in connection with the article on the Chinese was achieved by indirect statement. The other discrimination was contained in the provision that natives of China, along with idiots, insane persons, and persons convicted of infamous crimes or of the embezzlement of public money, should never exercise the privileges of electors in the state.[41]

On March 3, 1879, the constitution was adopted by the convention and ratified by the people the following May. During the two months intervening a very bitter campaign was waged, but the article on the Chinese had a very small part in it, the chief discussion being directed toward the articles on taxation and corporations. Most of the newspapers of the state were opposed to the constitution, the *Chronicle* being the only important one in San Francisco to support it. San Francisco, along with most of the other cities, voted against it, and the majority in the entire state was less than eleven thousand.[42]

Even before the constitution had been ratified the campaign for the election of state officers was under way. Including that of the "New Constitution" party, four tickets were placed in the field, all four including in their platforms declarations favoring legislation to restrict Chinese immigration. Largely because of the divisions among their opponents the Republicans elected practically their entire state ticket, including a majority of the legislature.[43]

Interest in the legislature centered in the measures for the enforcement

---

[41]The article on the Chinese is number XIX, and the other provisions are in Article I, Section 17, and Article II, Section 1. See *Debates*, III, 1519, 1510-1511.
[42]Davis, *Political Conventions*, 390-393. Swisher, *California Constitutional Convention*, Chapter VIII.
[43]Davis, *Political Conventions*, 395-418.

of provisions in the new constitution. Governor Perkins called the legislature's attention to the article on the Chinese and promised cooperation in any action taken, but expressed the conviction that only the Federal government could solve the problem. For several years the workingmen, more or less generally over the state, had been promoting a boycott against firms employing Chinese, with a view to substituting white labor. The *Post* had been the mouthpiece for this movement declaring, "Our policy of NON-EMPLOYMENT and NON-INTERCOURSE will empty Chinatown." This idea had been written into the constitution and the first act of the legislature was for the purpose of making this provision effective. It was passed as an emergency measure, providing that

> Any officer, director, manager, member, stockholder, clerk, agent, servant, attorney, employee, assignee, or contractor of any corporation now existing, or hereafter formed under the laws of this state, who shall employ, in any manner or capacity, upon any work or business of such corporation, any Chinese or Mongolian, is guilty of a misdemeanor . . . .

Not only were the penalties quite severe on individuals, but on second offense the corporation should forfeit its charter and all corporate rights and privileges.[44]

This act was passed and its enforcement attempted under tumultuous conditions. In connection with the state election in 1879, I. S. Kalloch, a prominent Baptist minister, had been elected mayor of San Francisco on the Workingmen's ticket. From the beginning of the Workingmen's movement Kalloch had made speeches barely less radical than those of Kearney, and during the election he became very abusive. While the bill forbidding the employment of Chinese by corporations was under consideration the Workingmen carried on a violent agitation, accompanied by daily parades of the unemployed and by threats, shooting, and conflagration. After the bill had passed they appointed a "Committee on Corporations" to supervise the enforcement of the new law. Officers of corporations in San Francisco were visited and demands were made for the dismissal of the Chinese employed, while violent language flowed on the sandlots.[45]

Within a week after the approval of this act it was on its way to the United States Circuit Court, which declared that both the second section of the constitution and this act for its enforcement were unconstitutional, being in conflict with the Burlingame Treaty and the Fourteenth Amend-

[44]*Acts Amendatory to the Codes of California, 1880; Penal Code, 1-2.* See *Post,* August 10, 1877, July 14, 1879.
[45]*Alta,* Feb. 11-17, 20-24, 26-28, March 10, 11, 17-19, 22, 25, 31, April 1, 4, 1880. During the election Kalloch and Charles De Young, one of the publishers of the *Chronicle,* engaged in a bitter exchange of personalities, and De Young shot Kalloch. The following April Kalloch's son killed De Young, but was acquitted. *Pacific,* Aug. 27, 1879. Davis, *Political Conventions,* 420-421.

ment. "Labor is property, and the right to make it available is next in importance to the right to life and liberty."[46]

Three other measures enacted during this session of the legislature received summary treatment in court. Immediately following Kalloch's election as mayor a special committee was appointed to investigate China-town, and an extensive campaign of renovation was inaugurated, with results somewhat better than usual. The legislature then enacted a law making it the duty of all incorporated cities and towns to take all neces-sary measures for the removal of the Chinese from their bounds. A second measure prohibited the issuing of a license for the transaction of any business or occupation to any alien ineligible to become an elector of the state, while a third prohibited aliens of this class from taking fish out of any of the waters of the state for purposes of sale. When several Chinese were brought into the Circuit Court in connection with the viola-tion of this last act Judge Sawyer declared that the act conflicted with the Burlingame Treaty because it discriminated between Chinese and other aliens, and violated the Fourteenth Amendment because it denied to the Chinese the equal protection of the law. He then referred to the other two acts and said that they were all of the same sort, passed with the same object in view, and equally unconstitutional.[47]

These decisions made ineffective most of the provisions of the Chinese article of the new constitution, within little more than a year of its ratification. Only one measure of this legislative session seems to have been allowed to stand unchallenged, an act directed against the control exercised by the Six Companies through their agreement with steamship companies. This act made it a misdemeanor for any transportation company to refuse any person a passage ticket on the ground that he had not presented a certificate showing that he had paid all of his obligations.[48] The following year the legislature prohibited the selling or giving of opium, or the visiting of any place for the smoking of opium.[49] To what extent these laws were enforced does not appear, but they represent the very meagre results from the new constitution, and it is not surprising that the anti-Chinese forces eagerly awaited the enactment of the first national restrictive law.

Political and economic conditions in San Francisco were of such character that it would have been surprising if, during the period follow-ing the ratification of the constitution, no new regulations governing the

---

[46]*In re Tiburcio Parrott*, 6 Sawyer, 349. Section three of the Chinese article had been made ineffective six months before the legislature met by a decision involving a similar law in Oregon. 5 Sawyer, 566-573.
[47]*In re Ah Chong*, 6 Sawyer, 451-457. The laws are in *Cal. Statutes, 1880*, 22, 39, 123. An attempt to remove Chinatown from San Francisco in 1890 met the same fate. *Bulletin*, Aug. 25, 1890.
[48]*Cal. Statutes, 1880*, 15-16. See *Report 689*, 176, 406. *Bulletin*, Oct. 11, 13, 1883.
[49]*Cal. Statutes, 1881*, 34.

Chinese had been adopted. The Workingmen, under the leadership of the new mayor, turned their attention again to the removal of the Chinese quarter. A special committee investigated Chinatown, reported anew the evils to be found there, and an extensive program of renovation was inaugurated. This agitation was influential in securing the passage of the law authorizing cities to remove dangerous aliens from their midst. At the same time the Workingmen promoted a movement for the election of freeholders to draw up a new charter for the city, better suited to the attainment of their objectives. But the Citizens' Protective Union sponsored a fusion ticket which defeated the Workingmen's candidates so badly that the leaders were almost stunned.[50] The Workingmen received a further setback in the conviction of Kearney and Gannon, and in the efforts of the Board of Supervisors to impeach Kalloch. These events practically ended the effective leadership of Kearney and of the Workingmen's Party.[51]

This defeat of the Workingmen, however, did not prevent additional measures against the Chinese. One ordinance made it unlawful for any person to maintain, visit, or let a building for any house of ill fame or for the practice of gambling. A second prohibited the maintaining or visiting of a place where opium was smoked, but this was changed the next year to a high-license system. The building of scaffolds on the roofs of buildings was forbidden, except with the special consent of the Board of Supervisors. It was made unlawful for any person to own any of the devices connected with a lottery, to visit a lottery or any place where tickets were sold or registered, or in any way to contribute to the maintenance of a lottery. The use of materials of Chinese production or importation in the building or repair of streets and sewers was prohibited, and ships were forbidden to land any person afflicted with leprosy or elephantiasis.[52]

In 1885, with a municipal election approaching, the Board of Supervisors ordered another investigation of Chinatown. An elaborate survey was made and a long report presented repeating, for the greater part, statements of conditions long familiar. The "Cubic Air" ordinance was reenacted and convicted violators were to be put to hard labor on public works; iron or unusually heavy wood doors were not to be used without a permit from the Board of Supervisors; fires in tin cans or other makeshift arrangements were forbidden; the stationing of guards before

---

[50]*Post,* July 9, 1879; *Bulletin,* Feb. 23, 24, June 16, 1880. *Alta,* March 31, April 1, 1880. The *Alta* was almost hysterical during the week preceding the election, and claimed most of the credit for the result.
[51]*Alta,* April 4, 6, 18, 20, 25, May 4, 13, 29, 1880. The best estimate of Kearney's contribution is, "He put the fear of the toiler into the heart of the politician." Claude G. Bowers in *The American Secretaries of State and their Diplomacy,* VII, 252.
[52]*General Orders, 1888,* 32, 39, 42, 65, 179, 192. These ordinances were passed during the years 1880-1883.

lottery or gambling places was prohibited; and property owners were forbidden to let their buildings for disorderly purposes.[53]

Chinese laundries had been a point of attack for many years, especially because of the light, inflammable materials of which they were constructed, the long hours of their operation, and the asserted carelessness of the owners in the use of fire. In 1880 an ordinance was passed requiring laundries to be constructed with stone or brick walls, only one story high, with metal roof and metal or metal-covered doors and window-shutters. Only with the consent of the Board of Supervisors could a laundry be located in a different kind of building. When this ordinance was amended to prohibit laundries in certain areas of the city, except under the most severe restrictions, the Federal court declared it unconstitutional because it tended to be prohibitive, holding that a laundry of itself was not against good morals or dangerous to public safety. These objectionable features were removed and a provision added forbidding laundries to operate between ten o'clock at night and six in the morning, and on Sunday. This was sustained by the United States Supreme Court as a police regulation within the competency of a municipality.[54]

In 1885 almost two hundred Chinese laundrymen were arrested and twenty-eight convicted of violating the ordinance against the use of frame buildings, and the state supreme court sustained all of the laundry ordinances. When the case was taken to the United States Supreme Court the ordinances were declared unconstitutional, on the ground that they conferred upon the Board of Supervisors arbitrary power and that the administration of the ordinances showed that, while Chinese who met the requirements were denied licenses, a large number of whites who had not met the legal regulations were granted licenses. The following year these ordinances were so amended that a license would issue upon a certificate from the Health Officer to the effect that proper sanitary conditions existed, and one from the Fire Wardens that proper precautions had been taken against fire.[55]

The laundry ordinances illustrate the difficulties encountered in attempting to deal with the Chinese problem through local regulations. They were a fitting climax to the period treated in this chapter. It began with an appeal to the Federal government, and then, because progress was slow and because new factors appeared locally, an attempt was made to deal with the problem through the new constitution, and by means of municipal ordinances. Most of these, in turn, were made ineffective by the Federal courts, and the anti-Chinese forces of the state were driven again to appeal to the national government.

---

[53]*Municipal Reports, 1884-85*, Appendix, 162-231.
[54]*Bulletin*, Aug. 25, 1880, May 9, 1882, Aug. 24, 1885. *General Orders, 1888*, 42. 7 Sawyer, 526. 113 U. S. Reports, 703-711.
[55]*Bulletin*, Aug. 29, 1885. 68 California, 294. 11 Sawyer, 422. 118 U. S. Reports, 356. *General Orders, 1888*, 199-201. Such provisions as had been upheld by the courts were retained.

One of the most careful students of this period has thus characterized the state and local legislation against the Chinese:

The legislation on Oriental labor sprang from the people. The centers of anti-Chinese agitation have always been found at the points of greatest contact between the two types of labor, hence the laws on the subject have not been of the type which far-seeing statesmen might suggest, and whose support is largely a matter of the education of public opinion. They were the product of the actual experiences,—sometimes of the race prejudices,—of those in the humblest ranks of society . . . . The largely instinctive judgment of the working people of California, which has refused to sanction this admixture of races, has been accepted as the policy of the nation. The origin of the anti-Chinese legislation is shown in the relationship which the different groups of laws bear to each other. The regulations made in the miner's meetings are repeated in the state laws and even in the Federal statutes; the demands of the labor unions are reflected in city ordinances, and these in turn suggested measures passed by the state legislature; while the futile attempts at state exclusion furnished the models for Federal laws regulating immigration.[56]

---

[56]Eaves, *California Labor Legislation*, 115-116.

CHAPTER V

THE ACHIEVEMENT OF RESTRICTION

As was pointed out in the preceding chapter, by the spring of 1876 events had convinced the leaders of the anti-Chinese movement in California that efforts for the legal restriction of Chinese immigration must be directed toward the national government. It is apparent, also, that by that date economic and political conditions in the United States were such that it had become increasingly easy to get a national hearing on the subject.

In order to understand the conduct of the Federal government in this matter it is necessary to take into consideration what had occurred in preceding years. Coincident with the close of the Revolutionary War, American ships entered the trade with China, which grew rapidly in importance through succeeding decades. Largely in the interest of this trade Caleb Cushing was sent to negotiate our first treaty with China. By the terms of this treaty the United States and its citizens were to enjoy all of the privileges which had been, or might later be conferred upon any other nation, including those of trade and protection, the maintenance of consular officers at the five open ports, and extra-territorial rights. Fourteen years later, profiting from the war of Great Britain and France against China, the United States secured three new treaties, renewing and expanding these privileges.[1]

None of these treaties was reciprocal in character, but in 1868 this principle was embodied in a new treaty. Anson Burlingame, who had gone to China as minister in 1862, returned as the head of the first Chinese mission to the treaty powers. Accompanied by two high Chinese officials and a numerous retinue, Burlingame was given a great banquet at San Francisco, attended by most of the leading citizens of the state, as well as the consular representatives of other nations. Proceeding to Washington, Burlingame and William H. Seward concluded a "Treaty of Trade, Consuls, and Emigration," articles five and six dealing especially with immigration:

> The United States of America and the Emperor of China cordially recognize the inherent and inalienable right of man to change his home and allegiance, and also the mutual advantage of the free migration and emigration of their citizens and subjects respectively from one country to the other for purposes of curiosity, of trade or as permanent residents. The high contracting parties therefore join in reprobating any other than an entirely voluntary emigration for these purposes. They consequently agree to pass laws making it a penal offence for a citizen of the United States or Chinese subject to take Chinese subjects either to the United

[1]Malloy, *Treaties*, I, 196-233. Foster, *American Diplomacy in the Orient*, 214-254. Williams, *Middle Kingdom*, II, 463-574, 625-689. For the earlier period, Charles A. and Mary R. Beard, *Rise of American Civilization*, I, 719-724. Moore, *Digest*, V, 416-426.

States or to any other foreign country, or for a Chinese subject or citizen of the United States to take citizens of the United States to China or to any other foreign country without this free and voluntary consent, respectively.

Citizens of the United States visiting or residing in China shall enjoy the same privileges, immunities or exemptions in respect to travel or residence as may there be enjoyed by the citizens or subjects of the most favored nation; and, reciprocally, Chinese subjects visiting or residing in the United States shall enjoy the same privileges, immunities and exemptions in respect to travel or residence as may there be enjoyed by the citizens or subjects of the most favored nation. But nothing herein contained shall be held to confer naturalization upon citizens of the United States in China, nor upon the subjects of China in the United States.[2]

The first of these articles represented a concession on the part of China, not in what it granted American citizens, but because it recognized the right of emigration, upon which the Chinese government had frowned officially, if not effectively for centuries. This article also committed the Chinese government against the coolie trade. The sixth article did not add to the privileges already enjoyed by American citizens in China, nor did it add to those which the Chinese could legally claim in America. What it did was to place a definite legal barrier in the way of any attempt to discriminate against Chinese subjects—a barrier which received full recognition from the United States courts.[3]

The treaty was cordially received by the people of the United States, especially by those interested in commerce and in the uplift of the colored races, both strong groups in the northeastern part of the country. In California, also, those who were interested in manufacturing and agriculture, in the draining of tule lands, and in transportation seem to have been pleased with the treaty. J. Ross Browne, Burlingame's successor, wrote from San Francisco:

There is no unfriendly feeling here toward the Chinese among the influential and respectable class of the community . . . . The objections against them are purely of a local and political character and come from the lower classes of Irish.

And the *Alta* added the comment:

The treaty rights an injustice. It administers another blow to the accursed spirit of caste . . . . The day cannot be far when some district on the Pacific slope will contain a majority of Chinese voters, and will elect a Chinaman to Congress.[4]

The labor groups on the coast did not regard the treaty with favor. Numerous protests were made against it, and before the proclamation of the treaty was six months old a state anti-Chinese convention made its abrogation one of the chief objectives. During the following decade the

---

[2]Malloy, *Treaties*, I, 234-236. Foster, *American Diplomacy*, 258-263. *Alta* and *Bulletin*, April 29, 1868. Frederick Wells Williams, *Anson Burlingame and the First Chinese Mission to Foreign Powers.* (1912).

[3]This principle of the right of emigration had been included in the treaties of 1860 and 1866 with Great Britain and France, and had been proclaimed by the Chinese government. Chen, *Chinese Migrations*, 17-18. It is not true that this treaty "opened the door of the United States to the Chinese." Rhodes, *United States*, VIII, 181. The door had never been closed.

[4]*Alta*, Aug. 31, 1868. Williams, *Anson Burlingame*, 153-154. Foster says the treaty was opposed by American merchants in China as an attempt to deceive the western powers. *American Diplomacy*, 266-268.

treaty continued to be a center of attack and its modification or abrogation an object of endeavor for the anti-Chinese forces. Even after the
first restrictive laws were enacted Californians could not forget this
treaty and its alleged connection with the coming of the Chinese.

> Mammon, masquerading in the disguise of humanity, patriotism, and national
> generosity, worked its way into our diplomatic service and gave us the Burlingame
> treaty.
> We charge that Anson Burlingame deliberately sold his country's birthright for
> Chinese money; . . . .
> It was conceived in fraud and chicane. It was negotiated at a time when no
> treaty was wanted by either country, and not for the purpose named in the treaty.
> It lays that down to be a public and natural law which never was, and never in the
> nature of things can be such. It is an international lie, patent on its face. It never
> ought to have been entered into.[5]

Even before the making of the Burlingame Treaty, Congress had
enacted legislation regarding Chinese immigration. For several years
American ships had been engaged in transporting coolies to the West
Indies and South America, and in 1862 Congress prohibited this practice.
How successful this law proved it is difficult to say, for a few years later
it was claimed that many American ships had been sold to Europeans and
transferred to the Peruvian flag for the coolie traffic, and it was reported
that the Secretary of the Navy had ordered the warships in the South
Pacific to use all diligence in stopping American ships engaged in the
trade. Evasion of the law was made easier by the fact that for four
years during this decade the importation of contract labor was protected
by a Federal statute and that such importation was not actually prohibited
until twenty years later.[6]

The suspicions of the national government in connection with the
coolie traffic were aroused by proposals at the Memphis convention in
1869 to import Chinese to take the places of ex-slaves, by the shipment
of Chinese to North Adams, Massachusetts, to break a strike of shoemakers, and by the report of Consul David H. Bailey at Hong Kong,
describing in lurid colors the methods used in the coolie trade and
identifying the Chinese immigration to the United States with this trade.
These conditions were brought to the attention of Congress in the annual
message of President Grant.

> In connection with this subject I call the attention of Congress to a generally
> conceded fact—that the great proportion of the Chinese immigrants who come to
> our shores do not come voluntarily, to make their homes with us and their labor
> productive of general prosperity, but come under contracts with headmen, who
> own them almost absolutely. In a worse form does this apply to Chinese women.

---

[5]Davis, *Political Conventions*, 498-501. Memorial of state anti-Chinese convention, 1886.
See also *Alta*, March 4, 1868, June 24, Dec. 1, 1869, July 16, Aug. 12, 19, 1870, April 6, 8, 1876.
Bulletin, Nov. 25, 1869, April 10, 1880. *Cong. Record*, 44th Cong., 1st sess., 300, 2158, 3087,
3763; 45th Cong., 2d sess., 3226, 3773, 4782.
[6]*Cong. Globe*, 37th Cong., 2d sess., 352, 555, 2938-2939; 38th Cong., 1st sess., Appendix
259; 41st Cong., 2d sess., 299-301. *Alta*, May 11, 1866. *Call* and *Post*, April 10, 1878.

. . . . If this evil practice can be legislated against, it will be my pleasure as well as duty to enforce any regulation to secure so desirable an end.[7]

Congress responded to this urging by enacting what is known as the "Page Law." This act made it a felony for a citizen of the United States to take to or from the United States any subject of any Oriental country without his free and voluntary consent, for the purpose of holding him for a term of service; for any person to import or to hold women for the purpose of prostitution, all contracts or agreements to this end being void; or for any person to contract, either before or after such illegal importation, to supply to another the labor of any coolie or other person brought into the United States in violation of this act or of the coolie act of 1862. American consuls in Oriental ports were required to board outgoing ships in an effort to enforce the provisions of this act against involuntary or contract emigration.[8]

The first general debate in Congress on the Chinese immigrants as residents of the United States arose in connection with the amendment of the naturalization laws. The need for changes had been emphasized by extensive frauds in New York City during the election of 1868, and during the discussion Representative Fitch of Nevada proposed to insert the clause, "any aliens except natives of China and Japan may become citizens of the United States." In support of this amendment Fitch and Sargent of California presented most of the arguments which later became so familiar. In the Senate, when the bill was within one-half hour of voting time under unanimous consent, Senator Sumner proposed a new section to read,

That all acts of Congress relating to naturalization be, and the same are hereby, amended by striking out the word 'white' wherever it occurs, so that in naturalization there shall be no discrimination of race or color.

Sumner, in the face of strong opposition, insisted upon having his amendment considered and the debate was prolonged throughout the following day which, being the Fourth of July, Sumner declared was the most appropriate day for this sort of discussion, since the Declaration of Independence held that all men were created equal. His motion, which received a majority on one vote, was finally defeated on reconsideration and the barrier against Chinese naturalization was retained.[9]

It has been pointed out in previous discussion that in the spring of 1876 anti-Chinese sentiment in California had been intensified by the increased number of Chinese immigrants, the annulment of California legislation by the Supreme Court, increasing unemployment, and the

---

[7]*Alta,* Aug. 12, 1869, July 3, 1870. *House Exec. Doc. No. 1,* 42d Cong., 2d sess., 194-210. Quotation from Richardson, *Messages,* VII, 288 (Dec. 7, 1874).
[8]*18 U. S. Statutes,* 477-478.
[9]*Cong. Globe,* 41st Cong., 2d sess., 4275-4279, 5121-5177. *In re Ah Yup,* 5 Sawyer, 155. During this same session of Congress the Civil Rights Act was passed, prohibiting the sort of discrimination represented by the foreign miners' laws and others.

peculiar opportunity afforded by existing political conditions. These factors quickly made themselves felt in Washington. Even before the decision of the Supreme Court was announced Senator Booth presented the concurrent resolution of the California legislature asking for the modification of the Burlingame Treaty, and Sargent, now in the Senate, introduced a resolution recommending that the President open negotiations for such modification as would permit the United States to restrict the immigration of Chinese.

Speaking for this resolution Sargent delivered one of his most bitter attacks on the Chinese. The idea that they might become citizens he dismissed rather shortly, nor did he have much patience with the humanitarian view regarding the Chinese.

The "enthusiasm of humanity" was a great moving power in the nation in 1868 when the Burlingame treaty was ratified. The national exaltation growing out of the emancipation of a race and the sorrowful events of the civil war, had its climax in the opening of our gates to all mankind.

He charged that the Chinese created unusual problems of sanitation and safety; that they subjected white labor to disastrous competition; that the vast majority of them came to this country under contracts of degrading service, involving the grossest frauds; and that the Chinese women were a source of social contamination, while the Chinese civilization in its entirety was unchangeably alien to our ideals and institutions. And since the Supreme Court had nullified all efforts to secure relief, the only remaining hope lay in Federal legislation. About two months later, after a rather lengthy debate, Oliver P. Morton of Indiana proposed the appointment of a committee which should visit the coast to find out "the character, extent, and effect of Chinese immigration to this country," and to report to the next Congress. The Republican National Convention had recommended such action only a few days before and the Senate accepted the suggestion. The House of Representatives appointed a similar committee, and the two were organized into a joint special committee.[10]

This committee opened its investigation in San Francisco in October, and during thirty days held seventeen meetings for the taking of testimony. These meetings were attended by representatives of the press, one representative of the state senate, one of San Francisco, and one of the anti-coolie clubs, Benjamin S. Brooks and Frederick A. Bee, attorneys for the Chinese, and one officer of each of the Chinese Six Companies. To guide them in their procedure the committee drew up a list of questions which indicate the scope of the inquiry.

---

[10]*Cong. Record,* 44th Cong., 1st sess., 2850-2857, 4418-4421, and scattered between 4507 and 5697. The Senate named Morton, Sargent, and Cooper, and the House, Piper, Meade, and Wilson. The last did not attend. A great deal of political wrangling accompanied these appointments.

1. How many Chinese are there in this country?
2. What is their moral and physical condition?
3. Do they come here voluntarily, or by what means do they get here?
4. For what purpose do they come? with the intention of remaining and making the United States their home, or of returning to China when they have acquired a competence?
5. Do they become attached to our institutions and reconciled to live and die here?
6. What kind of labor do they perform?
7. What is their character as laborers?
8. Do they learn trades and work in factories?
9. What rate of wages do they receive?
10. How does their employment affect white labor?
11. Do they prevent the immigration of white labor to this coast from Europe and from the eastern states?
12. What is the condition of their health and their habits of cleanliness and sanitary regulations?
13. From what parts of China do they come?
14. Do any sail directly from Chinese ports, or do they all come by way of Hong-Kong?
15. In what way do they live in this city?
16. How does their residence in localities affect the price of property?
17. How many have families?
18. How many Chinese women are there in this country, and what is their condition and character? Are they free, or are they bought and sold as slaves?
19. How many Chinese companies are there, and how are they organized?
20. Are they organized to make money, and in what way do they make it, or are they relief or benevolent associations?
21. What interest do the Chinese take in the politics or institutions of the country, and how many of them have become citizens of the United States?
22. What was the condition of these people in China before coming here?
23. What is the population of China as far as can be ascertained, and the general condition, manners, customs, and institutions of the people?
24. What is their religion, and what progress have the missionaries made in their conversion to Christianity?
25. What is their education, and their character in making and keeping contracts?
26. The condition of commerce between the United States and China; how it has been or may be affected by Chinese immigration.
27. What power has a state to prevent the introduction of prostitutes or vagrants from foreign parts?[11]

In the actual conduct of the investigation, of course, it was impracticable to follow this list. The last two questions were used only to point out the disadvantages of our trade with China and to emphasize the effect of the decisions of the Supreme Court upon California anti-Chinese legislation. All of the other questions may be condensed into six groups: the Chinese people, in China and in the United States; the conditions under which the Chinese come to America; how they live in the United States; Chinese labor and how it affects the whites; to what extent

[11]*Report 689*, 2-3. Senator Morton was chairman of the committee.

Chinese immigrants become Americans; and the moral and religious status of the Chinese. A very brief summary of the testimony under each heading is all that can be given within the scope of this chapter, and this will be open to the usual criticisms directed against generalizations.

The population of China was variously estimated at from three to four hundred and thirty-five millions. On the Pacific coast there were said to be at least one hundred and fifty thousand, most of them in California, and the number in San Francisco was estimated at thirty thousand in the summer and twice that number in the winter. It was generally agreed that the great majority were agricultural laborers from the Kwang-tung province, very young men predominating. There were a few merchants and a small number of women, but most of the latter were prostitutes. While most of the inhabitants of China could read and write a few characters, the proportion who possessed the equivalent of an eighth grade education was very small.[12]

Practically all Chinese coming to America embarked at Hong Kong. Some witnesses said the Chinese came on their own initiative, self-financed or aided by relatives; others said that they came under contracts to work for a definite period of time, like those of the coolie trade; more said that they came on money advanced by brokers at high rates of interest, contracting a part of their wages to pay for their passage. A strong difference of opinion arose as to the function of the Six Companies. The pro-Chinese witnesses claimed that these companies were benevolent organizations, with voluntary membership, and had nothing to do with the coming of the Chinese nor with their labor after they arrived. They admitted, however, that the Six Companies had an arrangement with the steamship companies to prevent the departure of members who had not paid all obligations. Those who opposed the Chinese insisted that these organizations were involved in the contract system, controlling the laborers after they arrived, if they did not do the importing. Employers stated that the hiring and paying of the Chinese was done through head-men, although the individual laborers seemed to be free. It was claimed that the heads of the Six Companies regulated immigration according to the labor market. In addition, there were secret societies, such as the "high binders," who handled a great deal of the traffic in Chinese women, as well as administering punishment for the violation of the rules of Chinatown.[13]

Almost every anti-Chinese witness who was given an opportunity emphasized the evils of Chinatown. Many of the pro-Chinese answered

---

[12]Report 689, 12, 26, 66-71, 89, 114, 156, 174, 236-241, 406-408, 445, 488, 497, 756-759, 831, 858, 942-948.
[13]Ibid., 23, 44, 76, 82, 93-96, 111-114, 121-123, 175-181, 224, 318, 404-406, 420, 445-448, 483, 511, 579, 591-593, 673-675.

this with the charge that the Chinese were no worse than some of the European groups, and that much of the evil was due to carelessness or corruption on the part of city officials. Insurance agents disagreed as to the effect of the Chinese on property values and on fire hazards. All who were asked agreed on the traffic in Chinese women for immoral purposes, although some asserted that equally notorious practices were being carried on with women of European stock. It was claimed that the "Page Law" had stopped the importation of Chinese women temporarily.[14]

No phase of the investigation received more attention than that of Chinese labor and its effects upon white workers. It was stated that Chinese labor was servile and therefore degraded white labor; that, having no families and a much lower standard of living, the Chinese could drive the white worker from any field; that the Chinese worker lacked initiative, but because of great ability as an imitator, tended to monopolize whatever field he entered; and that because of these conditions white laborers would not come to California. Others, however, asserted that the Chinese had contributed largely to the development of California in making it possible to introduce new agricultural products and manufactures, to build railroads and irrigation systems, and to drain tule lands, thereby creating more labor for the whites. They claimed that, compared with the east, California had no cheap labor, and that the widespread idleness among boys was due to trade union rules regarding apprentices and to false pride on the part of whites. They even asserted that Chinese were superior to whites because they did not get drunk and did not strike.[15]

Very few witnesses favored citizenship for the Chinese. Some held that the Chinese did not desire to become citizens, others that their lack of assimilation made them unfit for citizenship, while still others contended that if allowed to become citizens they would assimilate more rapidly. Some feared that, if given the vote, they would become the tools of their bosses or of unscrupulous politicians, while others saw great danger in having in the community a large group who could not be entrusted with the ballot. Some contended that their segregation was due as much to the barriers set up by the whites as to the natural attitude of the Chinese, while others ventured that if they would take up the dress and social habits of Americans they would have no more trouble. There were some who declared that the Chinese were so different from whites that they could not be assimilated.[16]

---

[14]*Ibid.*, 109-111, 126-138, 145-150, 208-215, 326-328, 405, *et passim.* A translation of two contracts was presented and verified by Gibson. *Ibid.*, 145, 405.

[15]*Ibid.*, 17-20, 75-83, 244-248, 264-267, 275-285, 313-316, 436-443, 504-508, 533-535, 553-558, 670-675, 723-738, 767-777.

[16]*Ibid.*, 103, 114, 188, 271, 286-294, 377, 435, 455, 508, 510, 538, 586-588, 678, 697, 811, 942, 1010-1012. The division of opinion was not on strictly pro- and anti-Chinese lines.

Questions concerning the moral condition and influence of the Chinese brought out the sharpest clashes of the entire investigation. It was charged that they were all inveterate gamblers, that the killing of female infants was a common practice, that they shielded offenders from the officers of the law, being especially notorious for lying and perjury, that they evaded the poll tax by substituting receipts, that they were generally unreliable, and that their prostitutes lured young American boys into immoral practices and exposed them to foul diseases.[17]

The defenders of the Chinese, however, seem to have had the better of this argument. They pointed out that drunkenness was almost unknown among the Chinese; the statistics of the San Francisco police revealed that in proportion to population there were no more arrests among the Chinese than among the other elements of the city's population; judges stated that perjury was very common among the whites, and Mayor Bryant admitted the same difficulty in enforcing the gambling ordinances on the whites as on the Chinese. It was claimed that immorality was as prevalent among Europeans as among Chinese, and that more money changed hands in gambling among whites than among Chinese. The reliability of the Chinese merchants was vouched for by the heads of some of the leading business and financial institutions of the city. The anti-Chinese leaders sought to show the futility and fruitlessness of missionary efforts and alleged that Chinese civilization had become so crystallized that christianization was impossible. Several ministers, however, claimed that there were probably as many conversions among the Chinese as among white adult males who had had no previous Christian training, and that the Chinese converts were as loyal as those of any other race.[18]

Altogether one hundred and twenty-nine men and women were questioned, including lawyers, manufacturers, ministers, former members of the diplomatic and consular service, policemen, farmers, public officials, men engaged in commerce, physicians, tideland developers, railroad builders and owners, laboring men and women, newspaper and insurance men, and a few whose occupations were not definitely stated. Without a doubt it was a much more nearly balanced group than appeared before the state senate committee earlier in the year. A year later the Chinese Six Companies published the names of twenty-nine of "California's Leading Citizens" who had testified in their behalf. Indeed, newspapers expressed the opinion that the Chinese had got the better of the investigation, and feared its effect upon the eastern part of the nation.[19]

---

[17]Ibid., 116-120, 187, 210, 223, 254, 274, 291, 298, 372, 736-739, 1020, 1062, 1129.

[18]Ibid., 89, 182, 189, 299, 372, 401-404, 413, 434, 443, 485-492, 508-510, 534, 542, 632, 652, 689, 711, 749, 853, 903-905. This line of evidence greatly impressed Senator Morton. Ibid., 157, 162.

[19]Nevada Transcript, Nov. 17, 20, 1876. Santa Cruz Courier, Nov. 24, 1876. Oakland Transcript, Nov. 15, 1876. Chronicle, Mar. 10, 1877. Memorial of the Six Chinese Companies. No Chinese were heard.

In general the pro-Chinese witnesses included former diplomatic and consular officers, ministers, and men connected with foreign trade and other forms of capitalistic enterprise, while those opposed were public officials, newspapermen, and laboring men. It has been more or less customary to impute purely selfish motives to the latter group, while those favoring the Chinese have been credited with motives on a higher level. Without in the least excusing the self-interest and the propaganda character of much of the opposition as manifested in this investigation, two considerations modify somewhat the usual estimate of those who favored the Chinese. One is that the diplomats, the bankers, and those engaged in trade did not come in contact with the working class of Chinese, as did the laboring men. The second is that those engaged in capitalistic enterprises were admittedly interested in the Chinese laborer because he enabled them to receive profits from their undertakings. It is very questionable whether the interests of the Chinese themselves received much consideration from either side.[20]

Due to the illness of Senator Morton the report of the committee was written by Sargent and presented to the Senate the following February. As we should expect from Sargent, the report was strongly anti-Chinese in tone. Due to the insistence of Morton, however, it recognized that, from a material viewpoint, the Pacific slope had been a great gainer from Chinese labor, and the employers, as well as the religious leaders, were represented as favoring their immigration. But laborers, almost without exception, and a great many lawyers, physicians, merchants, and others, were said to oppose the further coming of the Chinese. Chinese laborers, because of their low standard of living, had greatly reduced the level of wages and caused much unemployment. These conditions had aroused bitter hostility against the Chinese. They were not fitted for citizenship, and yet the lack of the vote deprived them of any means of protection. The only way out was to restrict their coming. The report recognized that this view would not go unchallenged. Some intelligent people in California considered the cheapness and docility of the Chinese laborers strong points in their favor. But even if they did add to the material wealth of the coast, the dangers from lack of assimilation outweighed this gain. The problem was too serious to be treated with indifference, since the Chinese were spreading toward the east. The report recommended that the treaty be modified so as to apply only to commerce, and that Congress enact legislation to prevent the large influx of Chinese.[21]

[20]Coolidge, *Chinese Immigration*, 97-108. An interesting example was Dr. Arthur B. Stout, whose testimony was very favorable. Some years before he had strongly opposed them, his change of attitude being coincident with the acquisition of a large Chinese dormitory, paying high rents. *Report 689*, 643 ff.

[21]*Report 689*, III-VIII. *Post*, Feb. 10, 1877.

Two minority reports came out of this committee. The first, by Congressman Meade, agreed with the majority as to the seriousness of the situation, emphasized the labor problem, and urged the negotiation of a new treaty, since he doubted the power of Congress to restrict immigration under the existing one. The other was that of Senator Morton, presented after his death. Pointing out that the fundamental principles of our government are contained in the Declaration of Independence, and that this country has always been open to all the world, he argued against a renewal of race prejudice, which he considered the basis of the difficulty in California.

If the Chinese in California were white people, being in all other respects what they are, I do not believe that the complaints and warfare made against them would have existed to any considerable extent. Their difference in color, dress, manners, and religion have, in my judgment, more to do with this hostility than their alleged vices or any actual injury to the white people of California. . . . . Looking at the question broadly, and at the effect which Chinese labor has exerted in California, running through a period of twenty-five years, I am strongly of the opinion, that, but for the presence of the Chinese, California would not now have more than one-half or two-thirds of her present population; that Chinese labor has opened up many avenues and new industries for white labor, made many kinds of business possible, and laid the foundations of manufacturing interests that bid fair to rise to enormous proportions; that the presence of the Chinese, holding out the prospect for labor at reasonable rates, induced the transfer of large amounts of capital and immigration to California, and of large numbers of business and enterprising men, thus making California the most inviting field for immigrants from every class of society, including laboring men; and, lastly, that the laboring men of California have ample employment, and are better paid, than in almost any other part of the country.[22]

For the greater part the document presents the more favorable evidence brought out by the investigation. Considering the relative influence of Morton and Sargent, it is not surprising that the anti-Chinese leaders in California regretted the publication of this document. The investigation as a whole made available to Congress and to the nation a large body of information concerning the Chinese in California, in which the views of both sides of the question were well represented.

The report of the investigation was presented to Congress in the midst of the Hayes-Tilden election controversy, which made the enactment of legislation on the Chinese question almost impossible. California representatives, however, continued their efforts to that end. During the preceding session the Democratic House of Representatives had passed two resolutions requesting the President to undertake negotiations with China for the modification of the treaty, but the Senate had not acted upon them. In the fall of 1877 labor disturbances made the problem more acute, and the anti-Chinese forces were disappointed when

---

[22]*Senate Misc. Doc. No. 20,* 45th Cong., 2d sess., 4, 9. Sargent expressed doubt as to its authenticity, and Meade wrote that he was surprised at its contents. *Call,* Jan. 31, 1878. *Argonaut,* Jan. 26, 1878.

Hayes failed to say a word about it in his annual message. The Chinese Six Companies had appealed to the President because of the threats of Kearney's group, and a representative of the commercial interests had told Hayes and Evarts that the Chinese were being misrepresented. Senator Sargent and Congressmen Page and Horace Davis communicated with the President and his Secretary of State to disprove these counter attacks.[23]

Criticised for lack of unity in their efforts, representatives of the Pacific slope held a caucus and agreed to concentrate upon one of several bills providing for a strict limitation of the number of Chinese who could be admitted. While Sargent, Booth, and Page urged the resolution for the modification of the treaty, Davis argued for the limitation measure. In addition to stressing the more important of the usual charges against the Chinese, Davis pointed to the experiences of other countries, such as Java, Australia, Siam, and the Philippine Islands, to prove that wherever they went the Chinese presented the same problems. He contended, also, for the power of Congress to restrict Chinese immigration, on the basis of a decision of the Supreme Court that an act of Congress may supersede a prior treaty. But Congress was not quite ready to take this step and merely invited the President's attention to the desirability of modification.[24]

Although this action did not meet their demands, the anti-Chinese leaders in California felt that they had achieved a real victory. They were elated over the change apparent in the attitude of the press and in the opinion of the nation, compared with the evident hostility of the previous year. During the summer hope of rapid progress in the negotiations was raised by the arrival of the first Chinese minister and the establishment of a regular consular office at San Francisco. It was anticipated that the treaty would be concluded before the opening of Congress.[25] But the Chinese minister seemed in no hurry to open negotiations, and when Congress convened in December apparently nothing had been done. However, the discussion was enlivened by rumors of plans for the extensive use of Chinese as strike-breakers in Chicago; by the denial of the Six Companies that they had ever imported Chinese laborers or received one cent of their wages; by the visit of Bee to Washington for the alleged purpose of working against the modification of the treaty; and by his reported statement that the opponents of the Chinese in

---

[23]*Alta*, Nov. 30, Dec. 17, 1877. *Bulletin*, Nov. 23, 30, Dec. 4, 1877, Jan. 10, 1878. *Call*, Nov. 24, Dec. 19, 1877. *Post*, Dec. 17, 18, 1877. *Cong. Record*, 44th Cong., 1st sess., 2158, 3087, 3099-3103, 3763. *Senate Misc. Doc. No. 36*, 45th Cong., 2d sess.
[24]*Cong. Record*, 45th Cong., 2d sess., 793, 1544-1553, 2439, 3226, 3773, 4328-4332, 4782. *Alta*, Dec. 23, 1877, April 19, 1878. *Bulletin*, Dec. 23, 1877, March 10, April 23, May 8, June 19, 1878. Sacramento *Record-Union*, Feb. 27, May 7, June 10, 1878. The decision was in the *Cherokee Tobacco Cases*, 11 Wallace, 616.
[25]*Bulletin*, July 2, 1878. *Post*, June 22, Aug. 30, Sept. 2, 1878, Feb. 25, 1879. *Chronicle*, Aug. 6, Sept. 29, 1878, Jan. 11, 23, 1879. F. A. Bee was named consul, with a Chinese consul general.

California should be classed with the extreme "Nativists" of an earlier generation and with those who had burned the depots in Harrisburg and Pittsburgh, and that the better class of California people preferred the Chinese to the Irish.[26]

If nothing had been achieved toward the modification of the treaty, at least Congress was in a mood of greater readiness to enact some sort of restrictive measure. The November elections had given the Democrats control of both houses, while the memory of the last presidential election and the prospect of another in the near future gave to the question peculiar political significance. Many bills were introduced, but the only measure considered was one which provided that no vessel should be permitted to bring more than fifteen Chinese on any one voyage. Accompanying this bill was a report arguing affirmatively the question, "Can Congress repeal a treaty?" After perfunctory debate, so controlled by Democratic leaders as to place the Republicans in opposition, the bill passed the House, all attempts to amend it being defeated.[27]

In the Senate, however, the bill was debated for three days. Chief among those speaking for the bill were Sargent, Booth, Grover, and Mitchell of the coast states, and Morgan and Blaine, while those who led the fight against it were Matthews, Dawes, Hoar, Edmunds, Conkling, and Hamlin. The bitter partisanship manifested in the lower house was almost entirely absent in the Senate. What came as a surprise to most of the senators was the fact that the negotiations with the Chinese minister could not be carried through, because he lacked authority to treat on this subject. Proposals to await further negotiations were voted down. After amending the bill so as to require the President to notify the Chinese government that the fifth and sixth articles of the Burlingame Treaty had been abrogated, it passed the Senate and was concurred in by the House.[28]

From the time when the bill passed the lower house it received a great deal of attention from the press all over the country. Such men as William Lloyd Garrison, Joaquin Miller, Henry Ward Beecher, and T. DeWitt Talmage either wrote or spoke against it, and religious groups sent in resolutions against it. In California the leaders of the Workingmen's Party disapproved of the bill as a political maneuver to win the laborer's vote, while some representatives of the commercial interests considered it unnecessary. But the constitutional convention, the chamber of commerce, the San Francisco Board of Supervisors, great mass meetings in several California cities, as well as eastern labor and legislative bodies, urged the President to sign the bill. When Hayes vetoed it on the ground that

---

[26]*Bulletin*, Aug. 14, Oct. 29, Nov. 3, 1878. *Post*, Aug. 12, 14, 30, Oct. 26, 29, 1878. *Call*, Oct. 30, Nov. 12, 1878.
[27]*Cong. Record*, 45th Cong., 3d sess., 361, 367, 447, 791-800. *House Report No. 62*, 45th Cong., 3d sess. *Bulletin*, Nov. 11, 1878. *Chronicle*, Jan. 2, 3, 1879. Sacramento *Record-Union*, Dec. 28, 1878.
[28]*Cong. Record*, 45th Cong., 3d sess., 1264-1276, 1299-1316, 1383-1400, 1796.

it would endanger the lives of Americans in China and violated our treaty obligations, Californians expressed disappointment and resentment, but there was little disturbance; rather determination, with confidence in the final outcome.[29]

The Fifteen Passenger Bill derives its chief significance from the fact that it marked a "turn in the road" in the immigration policy of the United States, for in spite of the veto, restriction was evidently only a matter of time. The anti-Chinese forces on the coast, therefore, immediately renewed their efforts. The newspapers published articles on the evils of Chinese immigration and sought to combat the "ignorance" of the east, especially the activities of such popular religious orators as Beecher, Talmage, and Joseph Cook. Both the Republicans and the Democrats held mass meetings, with Chinese immigration a major topic of discussion.[30] In Congress very little occurred during the following year, the leaders awaiting the modification of the treaty. George F. Seward, minister to China, was asked to secure the Chinese government's consent to a prohibition of the emigration of criminals, lewd women, the diseased, and contract laborers. Before the end of the year the President announced that the Chinese government had agreed to this. Seward's progress was not satisfactory, however, and he was recalled. In his place the President appointed James B. Angell, President of the University of Michigan, and with him two commissioners, John F. Swift of California and William H. Trescott of South Carolina, with instructions to negotiate a new treaty.[31]

After a journey featured by many delays the commissioners arrived in Peking near the end of September, and in the course of five weeks of conversations arranged a new treaty, the most important articles of which read as follows:

Article I. Whenever in the opinion of the Government of the United States the coming of Chinese laborers to the United States, or their residence therein, affects or threatens to affect the interests of that country, or to endanger the good order of the said country or of any locality within the territory thereof, the Government of China agrees that the Government of the United States may regulate, limit, or suspend such coming or residence, but may not absolutely prohibit it. The limitation or suspension shall be reasonable and shall apply only to Chinese who may go to the United States as laborers, other classes not being included in the limitations. Legislation taken in regard to Chinese laborers will be of such a character only as is necessary to enforce the regulation, limitation, or suspension of immigration, and immigrants shall not be subjected to personal maltreatment or abuse.

[29]Richardson, *Messages*, VII, 514-526. *Bulletin*, Feb. 10, 21, 25, March 3, 1879. *Chronicle*, Jan. 30, Feb. 18, 26-28, March 10, 1879. Sacramento *Record-Union*, Feb. 15, 24, 26, 28, March 3, 4, 1879.
[30]*Cong. Record*, 46th Cong., 1st sess., 2258-2263. *Bulletin*, March 12, April 17, Sept. 26, 1879. *Chronicle*, March 2, 3, 12, 13, 1879. Sacramento *Record-Union*, March 11, 19, April 5, 1879. James T. Farley and James H. Slater had succeeded Sargent and Mitchell respectively.
[31]*Bulletin*, July 27, 29, 1878, Dec. 3, 1879, March 25, Nov. 9, 1880. *Chronicle*, July 28, 29, 31, 1878, March 19, 1879, May 4, 1880. The reports of Consuls Bailey and Denny on labor in China supported California views. *Consular Reports, 1880-81*, 175-180. *House Exec. Doc. No. 60*, 46th Cong., 2d sess. Shortly after his return Seward published his *Chinese Immigration*, very favorable to the Chinese.

Article II. Chinese subjects, whether proceeding to the United States as teachers, students, merchants or from curiosity, together with their body and household servants, and Chinese laborers now in the United States shall be allowed to go and come of their own free will and accord, and shall be accorded all the rights, privileges, immunities and exemptions which are accorded to the citizens and subjects of the most favored nation.

The third and fourth articles assured protection to the Chinese in the United States against ill-treatment, and permitted the Chinese government to bring to the attention of the American government any phase of legislation which might work hardship on Chinese subjects.[32]

When Swift returned to California he said that the treaty "has untied the hands of Congress, and the matter of Chinese immigration is in the control of our government."[33] This seems to have been the prevalent opinion, and the anti-Chinese forces were confident of success. While the treaty was in process of negotiation the country went through a presidential campaign in which the Chinese question played a vital part. Both parties had declared for treaty modification, and although Garfield had expressed himself rather definitely in favor of restriction, the forged "Morey Letter" was credited with having given six of California's seven electoral votes to Hancock, thus emphasizing the political importance of the question. In the Senate the Pacific slope members held the balance of power, since the Republicans could control only when the independents, Davis of Illinois and Mahone of Virginia, voted with them. The question was taking on added significance, also, because eastern communities to which Chinese had gone were making complaints similar to those of California. Besides, California had sent John F. Miller to the Senate, a champion as aggressive as Sargent, and possessed of far greater tact.[34]

Of almost a score of bills introduced during the session of Congress following the ratification of the new treaty, the anti-Chinese leaders decided to concentrate upon that offered by Senator Miller. This bill, as passed by Congress, provided for the suspension of the immigration of Chinese laborers, skilled and unskilled, for a period of twenty years, exempting those already in the United States or who should arrive within ninety days after the approval of this act. It also prohibited the admission of Chinese to citizenship.[35] The principal debate, running through eight days, occurred in the Senate. Outstanding leaders, such as Hoar, Dawes, Edmunds, Platt, Hawley, and Sherman, spoke against the bill, while the leadership for it fell upon the coast senators, assisted by such

---

[32]*Senate Exec. Doc. No. 148*, 47th Cong., 1st sess., 24. For the negotiations see pages 6-33. See also Malloy, *Treaties*, I, 237-239. The treaty was proclaimed Oct. 5, 1881. A commercial treaty was proclaimed at the same time. *Ibid.*, 239-241.
[33]*Bulletin*, Jan. 10, 1881.
[34]Stanwood, *History of the Presidency, 1788-1897*, 405, 414, 416. Rhodes, *History of the United States*, VIII, 136. *Bulletin*, March 3, May 6, Aug. 14, Nov. 17, Dec. 28, 29, 1880. *Chronicle*, Sept. 16, 1879, Jan. 24, 1880.
[35]*Cong. Record*, 47th Cong., 1st sess., 1480. *Senate Exec. Doc. No. 148*, 47th Cong., 1st sess., 33-34.

men as Maxey of Texas, Garland of Arkansas, George of Mississippi, Call of Florida, Cameron of Wisconsin, Teller, and Bayard. Practically all of the old arguments for restriction were reiterated, while the opposition protested against the drastic terms of the bill and deplored the departure from the traditional policy of the American government, stressing the danger to the China trade. In the House the bill was passed without amendment.[36]

While the bill was under consideration supporters and opponents all over the country were active. More than a score of petitions and memorials were reported in Congress. All but one of those opposed to the bill came from New York and Massachusetts and represented principally religious groups and men interested in the China trade. Those favoring the bill came from various parts of the country, with labor groups predominating. The California Representative Assembly of Trades and Labor Unions sent an appeal to the workingmen of the country, summarizing the objections to the Chinese and urging agitation for restriction. The Republican State Central Committee became almost hysterical in an appeal to President Arthur, beseeching him to sanction any measure that Congress might enact.[37] In order that Californians might demonstrate their support of their Congressional representatives Governor Perkins proclaimed the fourth of March a legal holiday. Great mass meetings were held in more than sixty cities and towns and strongly-worded resolutions were adopted in favor of the bill. Senator Hoar was severely criticised because of his persistent emphasis upon the equality of races.

The Senator from Massachusetts attempts to revive the 'Fatherhood of God and Brotherhood of Man' doctrine, which met its quietus in California many years ago. . . . . Every son of Massachusetts in California is ashamed of him. Let him be ashamed of himself. . . . . The great chair of Webster is held, but not filled, by a dwarf.[38]

When President Arthur vetoed the restriction act there was deep resentment on the coast. This resentment was greatly intensified when it was learned that the reasons given for the veto were practically the same as the objections voiced by the Chinese minister, namely, that the twenty-year period and the inclusion of skilled laborers were contrary to the intent of the treaty, that the requirement of registration and passports was a violation of the second article of the treaty, that there was no provision for Chinese residing in other countries to cross the United States,

---

[36]*Cong. Record*, 47th Cong., 1st sess., 1481-88, 1515-23, 1545-49, 1581-91, 1634-46, 1667-75, 1702-17, 1738-54, 1899-1904, 1932-41, 1973-86, 2026-44, 2126-39, 2161-89, 2205-28. The New York *Times*, commenting upon the "notorious fact" that railroad lobbies were opposing the bill added, "How much of the sweet prattle about 'the land of the free and the home of the brave' was really inspired by selfish traffickers in Asiatic bone and sinew the world can never fully know." Quoted by *Bulletin*, March 24, 1882.
[37]"Petition to President Arthur on the Chinese Question." "An Appeal From the Pacific Coast to the Workingmen and Women of the United States" (1881).
[38]*Alta*, March 3, 1882. For the meetings, suggested by Miller, see *Alta*, March 3, 5, 6, 1882 and *Bulletin*, March 1, 4, 1882.

and that these provisions would prejudice the better class of Chinese against American trade. To Californians it seemed that the President was more responsive to the commercial interests of the eastern states than to the desires of the Pacific coast states.[39]

Immediately after the veto a new bill was drawn up with changes designed to meet the President's objections. The apparent intention of the Democrats to make political capital out of the veto probably influenced Republican leaders. Little effort was made to defeat the bill and very few amendments were made, so that the bill passed both houses substantially as it had been presented, and on the sixth of May the President signed it.[40] Following is a section-by-section summary:

1. Suspension of the coming of Chinese laborers to the United States for ten years.
2. Any shipmaster landing a Chinese laborer from any foreign port to be subject to a fine of not to exceed five hundred dollars or to one year in prison for each such person landed.
3. The preceding sections were not to apply to Chinese laborers in the United States on November 17, 1880, nor to those who might come within ninety days after the approval of this act. Exception was to be made for shipwrecked Chinese sailors.
4. Any Chinese included in the first part of the preceding section, desiring to leave the country by ship, was to be registered by the collector of the port, with full identification, a copy of such identification to be given to the Chinese as evidence of his right to come and go of his own accord.
5. The same provision was to apply to those leaving by land.
6. Chinese other than laborers were to be identified by a certificate from the Chinese government.
7. The penalty for any falsification was to be a fine up to one thousand dollars, or imprisonment up to five years.
8. Shipmasters were to furnish the collector of the port with a separate list of Chinese passengers.
9. The collector of the port was to board ships before the landing of Chinese passengers and compare certificates.
10. The vessel of any shipmaster violating this act was to be deemed forfeited.
11. Any person violating this act or aiding such violation was to be subject to fine and imprisonment.
12. Any Chinese entering by land without proper certificate was to be returned to the place whence he came.
13. Official representatives of the Chinese government were to be exempt from the provisions of this act.
14. State and Federal courts were forbidden to naturalize Chinese.
15. The term "Chinese laborers" was to include both skilled and unskilled laborers.[41]

In seeking to bring about the restriction of Chinese immigration by Federal enactment the California anti-Chinese forces were faced by two major obstacles: the traditional attitude of the United States toward

---

[39]Richardson, *Messages,* VII, 112-118. *Senate Exec. Doc. No. 148,* 47th Cong., 1st sess. *Bulletin,* March 29, April 5-7, 1882.
[40]*Cong. Record,* 47th Cong., 1st sess., 2810, 2967-74, 3262-71, 3308-12, 3351-60, 3404-12, 3532, 3777. *Bulletin,* April 7, 13, 15, 1882.
[41]22 *U. S. Statutes,* 58-61. The chief difference between this and the earlier measure was the shortened period of suspension.

immigration, as expressed in the ideal of America as a refuge for the oppressed of all nations, and the interest of influential groups in the China trade. Both of these interests had been written into treaties. The problem was complicated further by the fact that the great majority of the American people were quite ignorant of the conditions of which Californians complained, since the Chinese were not very numerous east of the Rockies. In bringing about restrictive measures full use was made of agitation and propaganda in numerous forms. But even more effective was the growing strength of organized labor, and especially the exigencies of national politics, which gave to the Pacific coast states the balance of power between the two great parties. Out of these conditions, after two measures had been vetoed, came the first law on the statute books of the United States restricting the immigration of an entire race.

Chapter VI

FROM RESTRICTION TO EXCLUSION

THE FIRST Chinese restrictive act, the culmination of years of agitation, failed to bring the results which Californians had expected from it. For this there are several reasons. During the year of this act California received the largest influx of Chinese of any like period in its history. Certain features of the act itself proved unsatisfactory. No provision had been included for Chinese in transit. Before the law went into effect several railroad companies inquired concerning the transportation of thousands of contract laborers from Cuba to San Francisco on their way back to China. After first ruling against it, the Attorney General decided that transit was not a violation of the act.[1]

Decisions of the Federal courts, interpreting the restrictive act, were at variance. Justice Field held that all laborers were included under the provisions of the act regardless of the port of embarkation, but that merchants and other exempt groups who were domiciled outside of China at the time the act was passed, and who came to the United States from a jurisdiction outside of China, need not furnish the certificate of identification. Judges Lowell and Nelson of the United States Circuit Court of Massachusetts, however, held that the act applied only to Chinese laborers who were subjects of the government of China.[2] In addition to these judicial and administrative difficulties there were charges of evasion by the Chinese themselves. The "Superintendent of Customs" at Canton was accused of issuing certificates in large numbers to laborers as "traders," "students," and "teachers." When these arrived, affidavits were furnished by Chinese residents to substantiate these certificates. Charges were made of conspiracy to evade the law, and the courts were soon filled with cases whose settlement in truth and justice presented baffling problems.[3]

Demands and plans for strengthening the law were not long in appearing. In 1884 the coming of Chinese laborers from any foreign place was suspended for ten years; the collector of the port was directed to secure from every departing Chinese the individual, family, and tribal name, besides the data for identification required in the original act; any Chinese not included under the classification of laborer must secure from the government of which he was a subject a certificate setting forth his status, with complete identification; the term "merchant" was so defined as to

[1]*Senate Exec. Doc. No. 62*, 48th Cong., 1st sess. *Statistical Review*, 34-35. During the seven months preceding Aug. 4, 1882, almost 27,000 arrived. *Bulletin*, Aug. 4, 1882.
[2]7 Sawyer, 536, 542, 546. 9 Sawyer, 306. 17 Fed., 634. 19 Fed., 490.
[3]*Senate Exec. Doc. No. 62*, 48th Cong., 1st sess. *Bulletin*, Oct. 15, 16, 25, Nov. 13, 15, 19, 20, Dec. 14, 17, 21, 24, 1883; Jan. 7, 11-27, 1884.

exclude hucksters, peddlers, and those engaged in the preservation of fish; the destination and financial standing of travellers were required to be on their certificates, which certificates were to serve as the sole evidence of the right of the bearer to enter; and penalties were provided for any substitution or falsification of certificates, including the deportation of any Chinese found to be in the United States illegally.[4]

This was the first of a series of acts, running through the succeeding twenty years, seeking to make the restrictive laws more effective and more inclusive. The goal of the anti-Chinese was exclusion, and they were aided in their efforts by the narrow margin between the political parties which continued to characterize most of the elections of these two decades. "No president cared to be on record as failing to approve such legislation, regardless of the critical situation in which diplomatic negotiations might happen to be."[5] This repeated legislation was stimulated by decisions of the Federal courts making the acts less effective than their proponents had intended. Administrative regulations were assailed for creating loopholes, and Secretary of the Treasury McCulloch was called "The Champion Nullifier" because of alleged laxness in enforcement regulations. The landing of Chinese immigrants brought serious charges of fraud and bribery, and the courts were criticised for permitting the writ of habeas corpus to be used for this purpose, a practice which was described as a "new and professional legal business."

> The future historian will find one of the most interesting chapters on the jurisprudence of the American Republic to consist in a description and analysis of the writ of habeas corpus as applied to landing Chinamen in violation, ... of the Restriction Acts in the United States courts of California.[6]

The revelation of these irregularities was followed by a new outburst of anti-Chinese sentiment. In September, 1885, a riot occurred at Rock Springs, Wyoming, in which more than a score of Chinese were killed. Shortly afterward the entire west coast became inflamed almost simultaneously. Tacoma burned its Chinese quarter, and Seattle, Olympia, and Portland might have done the same but for quick official action. In California developments ranged from new ordinances of regulation to the burning of Chinese quarters and the expulsion of the inhabitants. Among the localities where these actions occurred were Pasadena, Santa Barbara, Santa Cruz, San Jose, Oakland, Cloverdale, Healdsburg, Red Bluff, Hollister, Merced, Yuba City, Petaluma, Redding, Anderson, Truckee, Lincoln, Sacramento, San Buenaventura, Napa, Gold Run, Sonoma,

---

[4] *23 U. S. Statutes,* 115.
[5] Alice Felt Tyler, *The Foreign Policy of James G. Blaine* (1927), 255. *Bulletin,* Oct. 30, Nov. 8, 1884.
[6] *Bulletin,* Jan. 24, 1888. See issues of Dec. 9, 1884, Jan. 7, May 29, 1885. *Senate Exec. Doc. No. 103,* 49th Cong., 1st sess. Richardson, *Messages,* VIII, 390-393 (Cleveland). 112 U. S., 536-560.

Vallejo, Placerville, Santa Rosa, Chico, Wheatland, Carson, Auburn, Nevada City, Dixon, and Los Angeles. In San Francisco the leadership was furnished by the Knights of Labor and the Cigar-makers Union, using public meetings and processions and the importation of cigar makers from New York to take the places of the Chinese, while the boot and shoe makers adopted a distinctive stamp to make it easier for purchasers to boycott Chinese-made products.[7]

Only by very strenuous efforts were the energies of this movement turned into the more peaceful channels of mass meetings and memorials. During the summer a conference held in San Francisco, attended by the California congressional delegation, Federal judges and others, had planned a drive for changes in the restriction law. In order to control the increasing violence a state anti-Chinese convention was held in March, 1886, which sent to Congress a memorial containing the very strongest declarations against the Chinese. Pointing to the experience of thirty-six years this memorial declared that the struggle on the Pacific coast was one of life and death, of the very existence of the white race. America was claimed as a white man's country, and while the coming of European immigrants had been a great benefit, the coming of an unassimilable race would be a calamity. The demand for cheap labor was likened to that for Negro slaves a century before, and a republican government was declared to be impossible with one part of the population dominated by another. It decried the "sham sentimentality" growing out of the right of free immigration, and endorsed the boycotting of all who were employing Chinese laborers.[8]

Scores of memorials and petitions poured into Congress from all over the country, most of them urging more effective restriction of Chinese immigration. Several bills were introduced and one passed the Senate, but failed to come to a vote in the House.[9] Temporary defeat, however, only postponed the inevitable. Further stimulus was added when customs officials discovered letters in the possession of Chinese on board vessels, containing full instructions for evading restrictions. Former employees of the customs office confessed to having sent certificates to China to enable Chinese to enter, and the Federal district attorney discovered a syndicate of professional bondsmen in Chinatown. Several Chinese were indicted by the Federal grand jury. As official confirmation of newspaper accounts the Commissioner of Immigration reported that during the year

[7]Coolidge, *Chinese Immigration,* 271-273. *Bulletin,* Oct. 24, Nov. 2, 6, 7, 17, 23, 1885, Jan. 23, 26, 27, Feb. 2, 9, 10, 13, Mar. 1, 1886. *Argonaut,* Dec. 26, 1885.
[8]Davis, *Political Conventions,* 481-504. Most of the leading politicians of the state were present. Sargent and Bidwell walked out of the convention in protest against the boycott, and Senator Stanford wrote, "My remedy for the evils the poor suffer is temperance, industry and intelligence." *Bulletin,* May 26, 1886.
[9]*Bulletin,* Dec. 28, 1885, Feb. 12, 15, 18, March 12, April 6, 30, May 1, June 2, 3, Aug. 6, 1886, Feb. 11, 1887. Davis, *Political Conventions,* 515.

ending in June, 1887, more than eleven thousand Chinese had been admitted, and in the summer of 1888 seven thousand cases were pending in the Federal courts in San Francisco.[10]

As a result of the agitation of the preceding three years a new treaty was signed in Washington on March 12, 1888, and transmitted to the Senate with a recommendation that it be published because of public interest. The treaty contained the following provisions: For a period of twenty years the coming of Chinese laborers to the United States was to be absolutely prohibited, except under the terms contained in this treaty, and the Senate amended it to apply to the return of those not in the United States at that time, whether they held certificates or not. This prohibition was not to apply to the return of a Chinese laborer who had a lawful wife, child, or parent in the United States, or property or debts due him amounting to one thousand dollars or more. Such person, however, was required to deposit with the Collector of Customs, before leaving, a full description of his family or property in order to receive a permit to return, and such return must take place within one year after leaving, and the Senate added the provision that without such certificate no Chinese should be allowed to return. Chinese officials, teachers, students, merchants, and travellers, who were not laborers, were to be exempted from all of these requirements, but must present a certificate from their own government, viséed by the United States representative in the country or port of departure. The right óf transit was continued, and Chinese legally in the United States were assured all the rights and protection accorded the citizens of the most favored nation, except that of becoming naturalized citizens. Because of losses sustained by Chinese in riots the United States agreed to pay the sum of $276,619.75 as full indemnity for all claims. The treaty was to continue in force for a second twenty-year period if neither government gave formal notice of its termination six months before the expiration of the first twenty years.[11]

Although one member of the California press called this treaty a "Democratic Sell-out on the Chinese Question"[12] there can be no doubt that, as amended by the Senate, it marked a long step toward the goal of the anti-Chinese forces. The Chinese minister agreed with Bayard that the Senate amendments did not materially change the treaty, but the Chinese government deferred ratifying it. In September the Chinese

---

[10]*Bulletin*, May 18, Aug. 23, Sept. 21, Nov. 26, Dec. 6, 13-16, 19, 20, 1887, Jan. 10, March 26, 29, 30, April 7, May 18, 23, 1888. *Alta*, Dec. 15, 1887. *Chronicle*, Jan. 12, 1888. William F. McAllister, *Immigration Report, 1887*, 6. *House Report No. 255*, 52d Cong., 1st sess. The usual massmeeting was held. *Bulletin*, Dec. 29, 1887.

[11]*House Exec. Doc. No. 1*, Part 1, 50th Cong., 2d sess., 357-400. Richardson, *Messages*, VIII, 610.

[12]*Bulletin*, March 28, 1888. For similar statements see *Cong. Record*, 50th Cong., 1st sess., 6570. *Call*, July 13, 1888.

minister telegraphed from Peru that his government wished further discussion on three points in the treaty: that the twenty-year period was too long, that every Chinese who had once been in the United States should be permitted to return, and that the property requirement was too high.[13] By the time this communication reached Washington, however, measures were under way which went beyond the treaty.

In order to understand the actions of Congress in connection with this treaty it is necessary to remember that these events took place during a presidential election year, an election in which the balances were very nearly even. Congress was in session all summer and both parties were keenly alert for campaign material. Anti-Chinese legislation meant votes, not only in the three Pacific coast states, but among laboring men all over the country. For this reason, more than any other, Congress anticipated China's ratification of the new treaty in passing a law for its enforcement.[14]

This act repealed the two previous ones and provided that it should be unlawful for any Chinese to enter the United States, except as permitted by this act; that officials of the Chinese government, teachers, students, merchants, or travellers must present a certificate of permission and identity from their government; that these provisions should apply to all persons of the Chinese race, whether subjects of China or of any other foreign power, except Chinese diplomatic officials and their household servants, and that the term "laborer" should include both skilled and unskilled; that shipmasters should be required to present sworn lists of passengers, and should not permit a Chinese diplomatic official to land until the Collector of Customs had identified him as such; that no Chinese laborer, leaving the United States, should be permitted to return unless he had a lawful wife, child, or parent, or property or debts due him to the amount of one thousand dollars, and that in any case he must make application to the Collector of Customs at least one month before sailing, present a sworn description of family or property, and must return within one year to that one of six enumerated ports from which he departed. The decision of the Collector of Customs was to be final, except for an appeal to the Secretary of the Treasury, who was authorized to make all necessary regulations for the enforcement of this act. Any Chinese found to be here illegally was to be deported to the country of origin.[15]

Obviously, this act exceeded the treaty provisions, especially in the unlimited period of exclusion and in the regulations governing the return of Chinese laborers then in the United States. But even before it

---

[13]*House Exec. Doc. No. 1*, Part 1, 50th Cong., 2d sess., 400-403.
[14]Although Harrison was elected Cleveland's popular vote exceeded his by over 100,000. Stanwood, *op. cit.*, 483. The political character of the legislation is apparent from the debate. *Cong. Record*, 50th Cong., 1st sess., 6568-74, 7293-7310, 7322, 7692-7709, 7746-59, 7706.
[15]*25 U. S. Statutes*, 476. Approved Sept. 13, 1888.

had received President Cleveland's signature another and more drastic measure had passed both houses of Congress. On September 2 a London dispatch reported that China had refused to ratify the treaty. This immediately raised questions as to the validity of the measure which had just been passed, since it was based upon the treaty. A new bill, supplementary to the other, was presented in the House by William L. Scott of Pennsylvania, Cleveland's campaign manager, and rushed through without debate. In the Senate, however, reasons were given for the inordinate haste with which the measure was being enacted. Senator Plumb of Kansas quoted the New York *World:*

> The motive for this extraordinary haste is so transparent as to appear like a bit of comedy. . . . . Mr. Scott has now made arrangements to create popularity on the Pacific coast. This was the meaning of the bill yesterday. It was this which galloped it through the House without debate or consideration. . . . . The Republicans could have broken the quorum yesterday, but they, too, were as anxious as the Democrats to make votes on the Pacific coast.

And the New York *Globe* was quoted by Senator Teller of Colorado:

> Both Democrats and Republicans have manifested a keen anxiety to be first to take advantage of the rejection by the Chinese Emperor of the treaty which has been lately negotiated between that country and the United States, and to use the opportunity in such way as to win the anti-Chinese vote by proposing the most vigorous laws for the exclusion of the Chinese from this country.[16]

The bill thus hurried through Congress was short and explicit. It provided that it should be unlawful for any Chinese laborer who had been or at that time was a resident within the United States, and who had departed or should depart therefrom, to return to this country; that certificates of identity, provided for in the act of 1882, should no longer be issued, that those already issued should be void, and that any Chinese seeking to enter on one of them should not be admitted; and that all necessary enforcement provisions of the act of 1882 were to be extended to this act, while all parts which were in conflict with this act were repealed. Cleveland accompanied his signature with a long justifying message, which was something of a political document in itself. After calling attention to the racial antagonisms which had led to the earlier restrictive laws he added,

> It was, however, soon made evident that the mercenary greed of the parties who were trading in the labor of this class of the Chinese population was proving too strong for the just execution of the law, and that the virtual defeat of the object and intent of both law and treaty was being fraudulently accomplished by false pretense and perjury, contrary to the expressed will of both governments.[17]

Within two weeks after its approval this law's constitutionality was being challenged in the United States Circuit Court, which held the law

---

[16]*Cong. Record,* 50th Cong., 1st sess., 8332-33, 8500. The date for the *World* was given as Sept. 6 and for the *Globe* as Sept. 8, 1888.
[17]Richardson, *Messages,* VIII, 630-635. 25 *U. S. Statutes,* 504.

constitutional, although in contravention of a treaty, for acts of Congress and treaties are equally the supreme law of the land, the later repealing whatever may be inconsistent in the earlier. This decision was affirmed by the Supreme Court.[18]

The Congress following the adoption of the Scott Act, in which for the first time in sixteen years the Republicans controlled both houses, was rather quiet so far as anti-Chinese agitation was concerned. But enforcement problems would not permit the question to be ignored. In two of his messages President Harrison pointed out certain defects of the law which made its enforcement very difficult. Particular attention was directed to the northwest where Chinese, having landed at Victoria, were crossing into the United States. The Treasury Department had ordered that those who came over the Canadian line should be sent back to China, but the courts overruled this order, saying that they must be returned to Canada. Since Canada, however, exacted a tax of fifty dollars for every Chinese entering the Dominion it was impossible to carry out this ruling. Chinese were coming in over the Mexican border, also, inspectors reporting a veritable "underground railway" from Guaymas to the American line east of San Diego. Negotiations were undertaken with Great Britain and Mexico concerning the matter, but apparently without success.[19]

To remedy these defects two bills were considered by the fifty-first Congress, both introduced by Morrow of San Francisco. The first proposed a careful enumeration of all Chinese in the country, to issue to each a certificate as evidence of his right to be here, and then to deport everyone found without this certificate. This bill passed the House but was lost in the Senate.[20] The other proposed to exclude all Chinese except officials, setting aside those parts of the treaty which permitted merchants, teachers, students, and travellers to come. Many protests against this bill were received in Congress and it failed to come to a vote.[21]

The California legislature, however, could not wait for congressional action, and proceeded to pass the most radical anti-Chinese measure in the history of the state. This act forbade all Chinese except duly accredited government officials to come into the state, and required every Chinese in the state to register within one year after the passage of this act. In addition to other details of identification the certificate of registration was to bear a photograph of the owner and to be recorded in

---

[18]13 Sawyer, 486. 130 U. S., 581. The California legislature sent John F. Swift and Stephen M. White to Washington to represent the state before the Supreme Court. *Bulletin,* Feb. 9, 13, 18, Aug. 13, 1889.

[19]Richardson, *Messages,* IX, 34, 41, 109-110, 197-198. *Senate Exec. Doc. No. 97,* 51st Cong., 1st sess. *Bulletin,* April 18, 30, May 10, Aug. 22, 1890, July 9, Oct. 9, 16, 1891. *Chronicle,* April 7, 10, 11, 1890. Several attempts were made to land Chinese on the plea of citizenship, claiming American birth. *Bulletin,* Oct. 8, 1888, Sept. 26, Oct. 3, 1889.

[20]*House Report No. 486,* 51st Cong., 1st sess. Morrow seems to have had little assistance from the California delegation. Senators Hearst and Stanford were inclined to oppose restriction.

[21]*House Report No. 2915* and *Senate Misc. Doc. No. 123,* both of the 51st Cong., 1st sess. *House Report No. 4048,* 51st Cong., 2d sess. *Bulletin,* Aug. 6, Dec. 5, 8, 9, 1890, Jan. 7, March 5, 1891. *Chronicle,* April 3, 6, 7, 10, 1890.

the county where the Chinese resided. Ticket agents and conductors were required to demand this certificate before admitting Chinese to any means of transportation. It was made a felony to aid a Chinese to come into the state, and if a Chinese violated any law of the state his right to remain was to be forfeited. No Chinese was to be admitted into the state without this certificate and if found in the state after one year without a certificate he was to be deported.[22] More than a year later it was reported that no real effort had been made to enforce the act and that only four certificates had been issued. When an attempt was made to enforce the law the state supreme court held that the act was in excess of the power of the state and in conflict with the constitution of the United States, which gives to Congress exclusive power to regulate commerce with foreign nations.[23]

The fifty-second Congress differed very noticeably from that which preceded it. Not only was the House strongly Democratic, but the California delegation was almost entirely changed, with several members eager to propose new measures for the restriction of Chinese immigration. In addition, the first session preceded a presidential election and there was some question concerning the validity of the restrictive laws after May 6, 1892. No less than twelve bills for the regulation of Chinese immigration were introduced, and the House Committee on Immigration and Naturalization presented a report stressing the need for immediate action, calling attention to frauds and smuggling of Chinese as grounds for additional legislation.[24]

After a very brief debate the House passed a measure that was so severe that the only two members permitted to speak in opposition declared it a revival of some of the darkest features of history. The Senate, however, struck out all following the enacting clause and substituted its own bill, continuing all existing legislation for ten years with a few additional enforcement provisions. When the House refused to accept this substitution the bill was sent to conference. Some features of the House bill were incorporated, and after more debate in the Senate the report was accepted by both Houses.[25]

The Geary Act, as this measure is known, continued for ten years all laws regulating the coming of the Chinese; placed upon the Chinese the burden of proof of their right to be here; fixed the penalty for unlawful residence at imprisonment for not to exceed one year, to be followed by

[22]*Cal. Statutes, 1891*, 185-192. The five dollar registration fee was to be used for deportation purposes.
[23]101 California, 197. George W. Walts, *Fifth Biennial Report of the Bureau of Labor Statistics, 1891-1892*, 13-14. Bills totalling $1,019.67 were paid for lithographing certificates and publishing notices. *Cal. Statutes, 1893*, 137-138.
[24]*House Report No. 255*, 52d Cong., 1st sess. "Our people are in no humor to submit to any more patchwork." "The only true solution of the Chinese question is absolute exclusion." *Bulletin*, Dec. 22, 1891, Jan. 21, 1892.
[25]*Cong. Record*, 52d Cong., 1st sess., 2911, 2914-16, 3475, 3624-29, 3832, 3869-79, 3925. *Bulletin*, April 22, 1892.

deportation to the country of which they were subjects; denied bail to Chinese in habeas corpus proceedings; made it the duty of all Chinese laborers in the United States to apply within one year for a certificate of residence, those failing to do so to be deported; these certificates were to contain all necessary data for identification, and a duplicate was to be kept in the office of the Collector of Internal Revenue; and suitable penalties were prescribed for any falsification of certificate.[26]

The Geary Act was accepted by Californians as the best possible at the time, but disappointment was expressed because the "final step," exclusion, had not been taken. It was felt that transportation companies and eastern industrial and trade interests had prevented the achievement of the desired goal. Senator Hale was accused of being

. . . . convulsed with apprehension that if the bill were passed diplomatic relations with China would be broken off. . . . . But he had not the least sentiment for the people who are sufferers by the Chinese invasion.[27]

The Chinese minister in particular was taken to task for his objections to the legislation concerning Chinese immigration, and especially for finding fault with the registration requirement and the denial of bail, Californians asserting that Americans who wished to go into the interior of China were required to be "tagged" with a passport.

The Eastern newspaper donkey has raised his sonorous voice in sympathy and declares that the certificate means the tagging of men, which he seems to consider to be a revival of slavery methods. . . . . The tagging, so called, has been resorted to simply because they are such inveterate liars. . . . . They lie in the bail bonds. . . . . But when it was proposed to forfeit them, the bailors disappeared, as well as the bailees, like the baseless fabric of a vision. Neither men nor money could be found after the most diligent search. . . . . To say that these groveling semi-barbarians . . . . should remain, unregistered, while our missionaries and merchants in China are tagged, so to speak, is the height of absurdity.[28]

Within a few months it became apparent that the Chinese were planning to resist the enforcement of the new law. The heads of the Six Companies proclaimed in Chinatown that the Chinese were not to register, but to contribute to a fund for the hiring of lawyers to fight the law, on the ground of unconstitutionality. In New York a Chinese Civil Rights League was formed and held a mass meeting at Cooper Union. Its president appeared before the House Committee on Foreign Affairs in an effort to have the Geary Act repealed, and a case was prepared for a test in the Supreme Court.[29] The court rendered its decision on May 15, 1893, and held that the right of the United States, acting through Congress, to exclude or expel aliens, either absolutely or upon conditions,

[26]27 U. S. Statutes, 25. Approved May 5, 1892.
[27]Bulletin, April 22, 1892. See also issues of April 16, May 3, 1892.
[28]Bulletin, May 7, 1892. See also issues of March 22, 23, May 17, 1892. For the correspondence of the Chinese minister see Senate Exec. Doc. No. 54, 52d Cong., 2d sess.
[29]Bulletin, Sept. 10, 23, 1892, Jan. 17, 27, April 7, 10, 12-14, May 2, 5, 1893.

"is an inherent and inalienable right of every sovereign and independent nation;" that Congress had the right to provide a system of registration and identification of aliens within the country, and to take all proper means to carry out that system; and that the act of May 5, 1892, providing for such registration and for the deportation of those who failed or refused to comply with its provisions, was constitutional and valid.[30]

When news of the decision reached San Francisco the newspapers gave it full front-page publicity, while consternation and dismay filled Chinatown. The Chinese were reported as being incensed at the Six Companies for misleading them, and the Six Companies threatened to send the Chinese to Canada and Mexico. Because it was believed that Congress would extend the time for registration and because there were no funds for enforcement, no further proceedings were taken.[31] The special session of Congress amended the Geary Act, extending for six months the time for registration and making the requirements even more rigid and inclusive, closely defining the term "merchant" and including under laborers those engaged in mining, fishing, huckstering, and laundering.[32]

Almost constantly from the passage of the Scott Act the Chinese ministers had protested to the State Department and urged the modification of the anti-Chinese legislation and, at least while Blaine was in office, received few replies and almost no satisfaction. Blaine was interested in Latin America and agreed more or less with the acts of Congress. In connection with the passage of the McCreary Amendment the Chinese minister expressed a willingness on the part of China to negotiate with the United States, "to the end that all difficulties between such nations may be permanently settled and their honor, dignity, and friendship maintained and preserved."[33] The result was a treaty in terms almost identical with those in the unratified treaty of 1888. It was to continue in force for ten years, to be renewed for a like term unless one of the signatories gave formal notice of termination, and in effect repealed the Scott Act. In Article Five, which in the earlier document had dealt with indemnities, the Chinese government withdrew all objections to the recent legislation, and the United States granted to China the right to require the registration of American laborers in China and

---

[30] 149 U. S., 698-763. Justice Gray gave the decision of the court, and Chief Justice Fuller and Justices Field and Brewer gave dissenting opinions. Attorneys for the Chinese were Joseph H. Choate, J. Hubley Ashton (of the Southern Pacific), and Maxwell Evarts.
[31] House Exec. Doc. No. 9, 53d Cong., 1st sess. Senate Exec. Doc. No. 13, 53d Cong., 1st sess. Only a few more than thirteen thousand had registered. See also Bulletin, May 15, 17-20, 22-26, 1893. Street meetings were held and Dr. O'Donnell and Kearney spoke.
[32] 28 U. S. Statutes, 7. House Report No. 70, 53d Cong., 1st sess. In May, 1894, it was reported that 105,312 Chinese had registered. Bulletin, May 11, 1894. This is known as the McCreary Amendment.
[33] House Exec. Doc. No. 1, 53d Cong., 2d sess., 263. Tyler, Foreign Policy of Blaine, 256-261. U. S. Foreign Relations, 1889, 1890, 1892, 1893. House Exec. Doc. No. 54, 52d Cong., 2d sess.

agreed to furnish the Chinese government annually a list of all American citizens in China, except government officials and their servants. The treaty was severely criticised in California because it recognized the right of transit and permitted the return of Chinese with families, with debts owing them, or with property, and because it was feared that it would nullify much of the recent legislation in spite of the fact that the treaty expressly stated China's approval of it.[34]

For almost a decade following the ratification of this treaty the legislation on Chinese immigration was largely routine in character. When the United States annexed the Hawaiian Islands in 1898 Congress prohibited all immigration of Chinese into the islands, except as permitted by the regulations of the United States government, and also prohibited their coming into the United States from the islands. Two years later the registration provisions of the Geary Act were extended to the islands and the prohibition on Chinese coming from the islands to the mainland was reiterated.[35]

Early in the new century the question was revived, inaugurated by a resolution of the national convention of the American Federation of Labor in 1900, calling for the strengthening and re-enacting of the Chinese exclusion laws. The following year the Chinese consul-general argued the question with the mayor of San Francisco through the columns of one of the leading magazines.[36] The San Francisco newspapers immediately took up the battle.

> Our grievance is against the humble, tireless, mean-living, unalterably alien, field hand and factory hand, who cuts wages, works for a pittance and lives on less, dwells in tenements which would nauseate the American pig, and presents the American workingman the alternative of committing suicide or coming down to John Chinaman's standard of wages and living. . . . . Self-protection is the sufficient ground on which to base exclusion.[37]

But it was not to be a movement on the coast alone; organized labor and kindred groups all over the country could be counted upon to help in securing the re-enactment of the exclusion laws. Nor was the Pacific coast so unanimously in favor of exclusion as formerly; the years immediately preceding had witnessed a great awakening of interest in the Orient, and the commercial groups on the coast were not behind their eastern rivals in their eagerness to capture this market.[38] But the

---

[34]Malloy, *Treaties*, I, 241-243. *Bulletin*, March 26, 27, 29, April 4, 5, 9, 16, 19, 24, 27, May 1, 8, Aug. 15, 1894. The decision of an immigration official denying admission to a Chinese was made final, except for appeal to the Secretary of the Treasury. 28 *U. S. Statutes*, 390.
[35]30 *U. S. Statutes*, 751. 31 *U. S. Statutes*, 161, Section 101.
[36]*Senate Docs.*, 61st Cong., 3d sess., XXI, 79. The Federation urged the exclusion of all Mongolians, including Japanese, and the California legislature joined. *Statutes and Amendments to the Codes, 1901*, 940. Ho Yow, "Chinese Exclusion: A Benefit or a Harm," *North American Review*, CLXXIII, 314-330. James D. Phelan, "Why the Chinese Should be Excluded," *Ibid.*, 663-676.
[37]*Bulletin*, Nov. 18, 1901. Fremont Older was the editor. The *Bulletin* claimed the cooperation of the *Call*, the *Chronicle*, and the *Examiner*.
[38]*Bulletin*, Nov. 19, 20, Dec. 3, 1901. The San Francisco Chamber of Commerce openly opposed drastic exclusion laws at this time.

methods were to be very much the same. Late in November a state anti-Chinese convention was held in San Francisco and claimed an attendance of three thousand from all parts of the state. After listening to speeches by many of the leading public officials, politicians, and labor leaders the convention adopted a long memorial to the President and Congress, very much like those of earlier days, and also a series of resolutions demanding the continuance of existing treaties and the re-enactment of the Geary Law. The convention also appointed a committee of five headed by Mayor Phelan, to work for their cause in Washington.[39]

With this question assuming increasing importance in public discussion President Roosevelt himself brought the matter officially to the attention of Congress in his first annual message.

> With the sole exception of the farming interest, no one matter is of such vital moment to our whole people as the welfare of the wage-workers. . . . . Not only must our labor be protected by the tariff, but it should also be protected so far as it is possible from the presence in this country of any laborers brought over by contract, or of those who, coming freely, yet represent a standard of living so depressed that they can undersell our men in the labor market and drag them to a lower level. I regard it as necessary, with this end in view, to re-enact immediately the law excluding Chinese laborers, and to strengthen it wherever necessary in order to make its enforcement entirely effective.[40]

Altogether twenty bills were introduced to accomplish this end. The House passed a measure to continue in force all existing laws, including the voluminous administrative regulations of the Treasury Department. The Senate approved a similar bill, with the regulations omitted. After long consideration in conference a compromise was adopted, re-enacting and continuing in force all existing laws, in so far as they were not inconsistent with treaty obligations, and these laws were extended to all of the insular possessions of the United States.[41]

While this act was being debated in Congress it received close attention from Californians. Deep resentment was expressed toward the Chinese minister, Wu Ting Fang, for his outspoken criticism of the exclusion laws, and toward the San Francisco Chamber of Commerce for the telegram sent to Congress opposing the exclusion of Chinese merchants. Lobbyists for transportation companies, missionary societies, firms engaged in the Oriental trade, and for the Chinese themselves, were noted, and mass meetings were held to counteract some of these influences.[42]

In January, 1904, the Chinese government gave formal notice to the

---

[39]*Proceedings of the California Chinese Exclusion Convention* (1901). Also *Senate Doc. No. 137*, 57th Cong., 1st sess. Gov. Gage had urged this matter almost a year before. *Appendix to the Legislative Journals, 1901. Bulletin*, Nov. 23, 1901.

[40]*House Doc. No. 1*, 57th Cong., 1st sess., p. xviii.

[41]32 *U. S. Statutes*, 176-177. Approved April 29, 1902. Debate in *Cong. Record*, 57th Cong., 1st sess., between pages 3654 and 4792. Innumerable petitions were received from all parts of the country in favor of continued exclusion. *Ibid.*, 4161-64.

[42]*Bulletin*, Nov. 8, 27, 1901, Feb. 7, 9, 10, March 1, 1902. *Chronicle*, Feb. 3, 4, 6, 15, 16, 28, April 9, 10, 13, 1902. *Senate Docs. Nos. 162* and *776*, 57th Cong., 1st sess. John W. Foster, Charles S. Hamlin, John M. Thurston, Gen. O. O. Howard, and Maxwell Evarts were listed among the prominent lobbyists against exclusion.

minister of the United States of its purpose to terminate the treaty of 1894 the following December, which would be the end of the ten-year period for which it had been negotiated. This action placed the exclusion laws in a doubtful position. It was held by some that, since the treaty of 1880 provided only for suspension of immigration while the treaty of 1894 provided for its prohibition, and the act of 1902 continued existing laws only "so far as the same are not inconsistent with treaty obligations," the existing laws would lose much of their effectiveness. The administration, on the other hand, was quoted as of the opinion that the laws could be enforced with at least equal effectiveness after the expiration of the treaty.[43]

To remedy this situation Congress attached a rider to the deficiency appropriation bill, amending the first section of the act of April 29, 1902 to read:

All laws in force on the twenty-ninth day of April, nineteen hundred and two, regulating, suspending, or prohibiting the coming of Chinese persons or persons of Chinese descent into the United States, and the residence of such persons therein, including sections five, six, seven, eight, nine, ten, eleven, thirteen, and fourteen of the Act entitled "An Act to prohibit the coming of Chinese laborers into the United States," approved September thirteenth, eighteen hundred and eighty-eight, be, and the same are hereby, re-enacted, extended, and continued, without modification, limitation, or condition; and said laws shall also apply to the island territory under the jurisdiction of the United States, and prohibit the immigration of Chinese laborers, not citizens of the United States, from such island territory to the mainland territory of the United States, whether in such island territory at the time of cession or not, and from one portion of the island territory of the United States to another portion of said island territory: *Provided, however,* That said laws shall not apply to the transit of Chinese laborers from one island to another island of the same group; and any islands within the jurisdiction of any State or the district of Alaska shall be considered a part of the mainland under this section.[44]

After twenty-five years of Federal legislation for the regulation of Chinese immigration into the United States, involving the negotiation of three treaties and the enactment of eight laws, there remained the treaty of 1880, parts of the act of September 13, 1888, the Geary Act of 1892 with the McCreary Amendment, and the act of 1902, all indefinitely and unconditionally re-enacted and continued in the amendment of 1904. The practical effect was to prohibit the coming of all Chinese except government officials, merchants, teachers, students, and travellers; to permit the return of registered Chinese laborers who possessed family or property; to extend these restrictions to the island territories of the United States; and to give authority to the executive branch of the government to make any and all regulations deemed necessary for the effective enforcement of these laws.[45]

---

[43]*House Doc. No. 1,* 58th Cong., 3d sess., 117-118. *Bulletin,* April 8, 9, 1904.
[44]33 *U. S. Statutes,* 428. Approved April 27, 1904. *Cong. Record,* 58th Cong., 2d sess., 5031-37, 5413-20, 5534, 5628, 5662.
[45]See 142 Fed., 128 for the significance of the acts of 1902 and 1904. Decisions upholding these laws are in 185 U. S., 213, 306; 186 U. S., 193.

SUMMARY AND CONCLUSIONS

CHINESE IMMIGRATION was merely one phase of that larger movement by which this continent has become populated with non-aboriginal peoples, and any peculiarities incident to their coming may best be explained by differences in the races themselves.

The chief motive actuating the Chinese in coming to the United States was the opportunity for economic gain. In the beginning it was the lure of the "golden hills" where, either as independent prospectors or in the hire of others, there were possibilities of income far surpassing the usual earnings in the homeland. When the mines became relatively less important the Chinese laborers found ready employment in new enterprises, such as manufacturing, farming, horticulture, railroad building, and the draining of tule lands. Their coming was stimulated by the ease of transportation, for passage was cheaper from Hong Kong to San Francisco than from New York or Chicago. Besides, the ship companies sought by advertising to increase the number of immigrants. The motives of political and religious liberty, important factors in European immigration, seem to have been almost totally absent.

For the most part the conditions under which the Chinese came were similar to those of Europeans, with a much larger proportion of assisted immigration. Thousands of them were imported by companies, both Chinese and American, which had contracted to supply laborers for capitalistic enterprises. It should be remembered, however, that this procedure was not in violation of American laws until near the end of the century. To what extent this importation corresponded with the prohibited "coolie trade" is an unsettled question. There is evidence that during the first few years Chinese were brought into California under "coolie" contracts, and it appears certain that the Chinese laborers were under the supervision of the Six Companies. Control was made easier by the practice of hiring them in gangs under "headmen," similar to the "padrone" system developed in connection with European immigration. Two observations are appropriate here. What appeared as servitude to Americans, especially just after the Civil War, was probably regarded by the Chinese as merely a means of securing employment; on the other hand, the absence of written contracts becomes less conclusive evidence in regard to the existence of obligation, in view of the binding force of custom in Chinese business and jurisprudence.

Diverse motives entered into the opposition of Californians to the Chinese. Fundamental to all of them was the antagonism of race, reinforced by economic competition. Principles of "nativism" found numerous adherents in California. If we can postulate an established moral standard it must be said that Chinese immoralities were little worse,

essentially, than those of Americans. But they were different, and therefore seemed more reprehensible. Race entered into the opposition on
the ground of unequal competition in labor, also, for the chief danger
arose from a lower standard of living developed through generations of
meager income. Coming at a time when wage levels in California were
higher than in the rest of the country, and when labor was maturing
its organization for the purpose of maintaining and even raising these
standards, the Chinese appeared to be the very embodiment of defeat and
disaster. Crowded and unsanitary living conditions, lack of assimilation,
perjury to escape punishment, as well as other vices, were not only out-
growths of the customary living of the Chinese, but were emphasized by
their opponents chiefly for the purpose of strengthening their case against
them, rather than because the practices themselves were obnoxious.

In true frontier fashion Californians attempted to solve the problems
arising from the presence of the Chinese by local measures. The first
of these were taken by mining districts and by the legislature, where the
mining interests were strongly represented. Later, as the economic center
of gravity shifted, ordinances were adopted by the cities, with the legislature still a responsive auxiliary. Poll taxes, license taxes on miners,
fishermen, and laundrymen, measures regulating sleeping quarters,
theaters, the location, construction, and operation of places of business,
of recreation, and of indulgence, and even measures to regulate the admission of Chinese to the state were enacted. These efforts at local control
reached a climax in the second constitutional convention and in the legislation enacted immediately following, with a belated outburst more than
a decade afterward. These legislative actions were preceded or accompanied by mass meetings, investigations, and riots or other extra-legal
endeavors, all of them enlivened by full description and discussion in the
press. Nearly all of these efforts, however, proved ineffective, either
because of difficulties connected with their enforcement or because the
courts, both state and federal, would not sustain them.

Failing in their attempts at local regulation, Californians opposed to
the Chinese appealed to the national government. One of the chief obstacles to local regulation was the Burlingame Treaty, whose terms
guaranteed to the Chinese the same treatment that was accorded the
subjects or citizens of the most favored nation. This treaty, as well as
those preceding it, had been negotiated in the interest of commerce, and
the groups engaged in this trade proved to be the most persistent opponents of legislation restricting the coming of Chinese to the United States.
Working to the same end were those imbued with the spirit which had
given Negro slaves equal rights with white citizens, and religious bodies
which promoted missionary activities in China. But the anti-Chinese
groups found strong support in the growing labor organizations of the

country, and in the south after the use of Chinese labor there had proved unsatisfactory. But the most effective ally of the anti-Chinese forces was the national political situation during the last quarter of the century. During this period two presidents were elected by minorities in popular votes and two others by majorities of less than twenty-five thousand, and the control of both the presidency and the two houses of Congress shifted frequently between the two great parties. Under these conditions the votes of the Pacific coast states came to be looked upon as of crucial importance, giving these states tremendous bargaining power in political campaigns. As a result men who were interested primarily in party success championed legislative measures which they otherwise might have opposed.

The California anti-Chinese groups began with petitions for the abrogation or modification of the Burlingame Treaty and proceeded by various stages to demands for the absolute exclusion of all Chinese immigration. Apparently reluctant to make these changes in national policy, Congress moved slowly. Before any action was taken, a fairly exhaustive investigation was conducted which resulted, however, in rather equivocal findings. After a bill for the limitation of Chinese immigration had been vetoed, a new treaty was negotiated permitting the suspension of the immigration of Chinese laborers. After a bill for the enforcement of this treaty had been vetoed, another was passed and approved in 1882. During the following twenty years six other acts were passed and two treaties were negotiated for the purpose of making restriction more inclusive and more effective.

In 1904 all existing legislation, extended to include the insular possessions of the United States, was indefinitely and unconditionally re-enacted and continued. By this action all Chinese laborers were prohibited from coming into the United States and its territories; those already here were permitted to leave and return only if they were registered and possessed family or property in this country; and merchants, teachers, students, and travellers were permitted to enter only under strict regulations. By that date the attention of Californians was being diverted from the Chinese to the Japanese, while nationally the exclusion of the Chinese was being submerged in the larger movement for the restriction of all immigration.

BIBLIOGRAPHY

BIBLIOGRAPHIES

Cowan, Robert Ernest, and Dunlop, Boutwell, *Bibliography of the Chinese Question in the United States.* San Francisco, 1909.
Griffin, Appleton Prentiss Clark, *Select List of References on Chinese Immigration.* Washington, 1904.

GOVERNMENT PUBLICATIONS: FEDERAL
Congressional Globe

37th Congress, 2nd session, 1861-1862.
38th Congress, 1st session, 1863-1864.
41st Congress, 2nd session, 1869-1870.

Congressional Record

43rd Congress, 2nd session, 1874-1875.
44th Congress, 1st and 2nd sessions, 1875-1877.
45th Congress, 2nd and 3rd sessions, 1877-1879.
46th Congress, 1st, 2nd, and 3rd sessions, 1879-1881.
47th Congress, 1st session, 1881-1882.
48th Congress, 1st session, 1883-1884.
49th Congress, 1st session, 1885-1886.
50th Congress, 1st session, 1887-1888.
51st Congress, 1st session, 1889-1890.
52nd Congress, 1st session, 1891-1892.
53rd Congress, 1st session, 1893.
55th Congress, 2nd session, 1897-1898.
57th Congress, 1st session, 1901-1902.
58th Congress, 2nd session, 1903-1904.

Congressional Documents

Note.—Serial numbers are shown in parentheses.
33rd Congress, 1st session, 1853-1854:
  House Executive Document No. 123, Correspondence of Commissioner to China. (734)
34th Congress, 1st session, 1855-1856:
  Senate Executive Document No. 99, Slave and Coolie Trade. (824)
  House Executive Document No. 105, Slave and Coolie Trade. (859)
35th Congress, 2nd session, 1858-1859:
  Senate Executive Document No. 22, Correspondence of Commissioners to China. (982)
36th Congress, 1st session, 1859-1860:
  Senate Executive Document No. 30, Correspondence of Commissioners to China. (1032)
  House Executive Document No. 88, Correspondence on Chinese Coolie Trade. (1057)
  House Report No. 443, Coolie Trade. (1069)
37th Congress, 2nd session, 1861-1862:
  House Executive Document No. 16, Correspondence on Asiatic Coolie Trade. (1127)
38th Congress, 1st session, 1863-1864:
  Senate Report No. 15, Encouragement of Immigration. (1178)
39th Congress, 2nd session, 1866-1867:
  Senate Executive Document No. 2, Report of D. A. Wells, Special Commissioner of Revenue. (1276)

41st Congress, 2nd session, 1869-1870:
  Senate Executive Document No. 116, Coolie Trade. (1407)
42nd Congress, 2nd session, 1871-1872:
  House Executive Document No. 1, Foreign Relations, 1871. (1502)
  House Executive Document No. 207. Re-indenture or Re-enslavement of
    Chinamen in Cuba. (1513)
  House Miscellaneous Document No. 120. Resolutions of California Legislature
    on Burlingame Treaty. (1526)
42nd Congress, 3rd session, 1872-1873:
  House Miscellaneous Document No. 81. Pennsylvania Petition against Chinese
    Laborers. (1572)
43rd Congress, 1st session, 1873-1874:
  House Executive Document No. 1, Foreign Relations, 1873. (1594)
  House Miscellaneous Document No. 204, Resolutions of California Legislature
    on Chinese Immigration. (1619)
43rd Congress, 2nd session, 1874-1875:
  House Executive Document No. 1, Foreign Relations, 1874. (1634)
44th Congress, 1st session, 1875-1876:
  House Executive Document No. 1, Foreign Relations, 1875. (1672)
44th Congress, 2nd session, 1876-1877:
  Senate Report No. 689, Joint Special Committee on Chinese. (1734)
45th Congress, 1st session, 1877:
  House Miscellaneous Document No. 9, Address of California Senate. (1774)
45th Congress, 2nd session, 1877-1878:
  Senate Miscellaneous Document No. 20, Views of Oliver P. Morton. (1785)
  Senate Miscellaneous Document No. 36, Argument of Joseph C. G. Kennedy.
    (1786)
  House Miscellaneous Document No. 10, Accusations against George F. Seward.
    (1815)
  House Miscellaneous Document No. 20, Resolutions of California Legislature
    on Burlingame Treaty. (1815)
  House Report No. 240, Chinese Immigration. (1822)
45th Congress, 3rd session, 1878-1879:
  House Executive Document No. 1, Foreign Relations, 1878. (1842)
  House Executive Document No. 102, Veto of Chinese immigration Bill. (1858)
  House Report No. 62, Chinese Immigration. (1866)
  House Report No. 111, Chinese Immigration. (1866)
46th Congress, 2nd session, 1879-1880:
  House Executive Document No. 60, Expatriation and Slavery in China. (1925)
  House Executive Document No. 70, Diplomatic Correspondence on Chinese
    Immigration. (1925)
  House Miscellaneous Document No. 5, Depression in Business and Chinese
    Immigration. (1928)
  House Report No. 572, Chinese Immigration and Depression. (1935)
46th Congress, 3rd session, 1880-1881:
  House Executive Document No. 1, Foreign Relations, 1880. (1951)
47th Congress, 1st session, 1881-1882:
  Senate Executive Document No. 148, Veto Message of President Arthur.
    (1990)
  Senate Executive Document No. 175, Instruction to United States Minister in
    China. (1991)
  House Executive Document No. 1, Foreign Relations, 1881. (2009)
  House Report No. 67, Chinese immigration. (2065)
  House Report No. 1017 Chinese Immigration. (2068)
47th Congress, 2nd session, 1882-1883:
  House Miscellaneous Document No. 13, Tenth Census: Population. (2129)

48th Congress, 1st session, 1883-1884:
  Senate Executive Document No. 62, Secretary of Treasury on Treaty Stipulations. (2165)
  House Report No. 614, Chinese Treaty Stipulations. (2254)
48th Congress, 2nd session, 1884-1885:
  House Executive Document No. 214, Interpretation of Restrictive laws. (2303)
49th Congress, 1st session, 1885-1886:
  Senate Executive Document No. 103, Fraudulent Importation of Chinese. (2340)
  Senate Executive Document No. 118, Correspondence on Treaty Rights of Chinese. (2340)
  Senate Miscellaneous Document No. 107, Memorial of California Anti-Chinese Convention, 1886. (2346)
  House Executive Document No. 102, Treaty Stipulations on the Chinese Question. (2398)
  House Report No. 2043, In relation to Chinese Restriction. (2441)
50th Congress, 1st session, 1887-1888:
  Senate Executive Document No. 115, Treaty Stipulations. (2510)
  Senate Executive Documents Nos. 272 and 275, Treaty Stipulations. (2514)
  Senate Executive Document No. 273, Approval of Exclusion Bill. (2514)
  Senate Miscellaneous Document No. 90, Statistics of Arrivals and Departures, San Francisco. (2516)
  House Miscellaneous Document No. 572, Contract Labor Law. (2579)
50th Congress, 2nd session, 1888-1889:
  Senate Executive Document No. 47, Information concerning Convention with China. (2610)
  House Executive Document No. 1. Foreign Relations, 1888. (2626)
51st Congress, 1st session, 1889-1890:
  Senate Executive Document No. 41, Execution of Exclusion Laws. (2682)
  Senate Executive Document No. 97. Arrivals of Chinese. (2686)
  Senate Executive Document No. 106, Chinese in Transit. (2686)
  Senate Miscellaneous Document No. 123, Remonstrance of Board of Foreign Missions, Enumeration of Chinese. (2698)
  House Report No. 486, Enumeration of Chinese. (2808)
  House Report No. 1925, Chinese laborers from Canada and Mexico. (2812)
  House Report No. 2915, Restriction of Chinese Immigration. (2815)
51st Congress, 2nd session, 1890-1891:
  House Executive Document No. 1, Foreign Relations, 1890. (2830)
  House Report No. 4048, Chinese Immigration, Select Committee. (2890)
52nd Congress, 1st session, 1891-1892:
  Senate Executive Document No. 98, Rejection of Henry W. Blair. (2901)
  Senate Miscellaneous Document No. 67, Report of Datus E. Coon on Chinese. (2904)
  Senate Miscellaneous Document No. 138, Memorial of Universal Peace Union. (2907)
  House Executive Document No. 244, Execution of Exclusion Laws. (2957)
  House Report No. 255, Need of New Exclusion Legislation. (3042)
  House Report No. 407, Exclusion of Chinese. Minority Report. (3043)
52nd Congress, 2nd session, 1892-1893:
  Senate Executive Document No. 54, Diplomatic Correspondence on Chinese Exclusion Laws. (3056)
  Senate Report No. 1333, Committee on Immigration. (3073)
  House Executive Document No. 1, Foreign Relations, 1892. (3076)
53rd Congress, 1st session, 1893:
  Senate Executive Document No. 13, Cost of Enforcing Chinese Exclusion Law. (3144)
  Senate Executive Document No. 31, Extending Time for Registration. (3144)

House Executive Documents Nos. 9 and 10, Enforcement of Geary Law, 1893. (3150)
House Report No. 70, Need of Amending Chinese Exclusion Law. (3157)
53rd Congress, 2nd session, 1893-1894:
   Senate Executive Document No. 111, Appropriation for Enforcement of Exclusion Law. (3163)
   House Executive Document No. 1, Foreign Relations, 1893. (3197)
   House Executive Document No. 86, Enforcement Costs, 1894. (3223)
   House Executive Document No. 152, Chinese Registration. (3226)
   House Report No. 618, Appropriation, Chinese Registration. (3270)
53rd Congress, 3rd session, 1894-1895:
   House Executive Document No. 1, Foreign Relations, 1894. (3292)
54th Congress, 1st session, 1895-1896:
   House Document No. 372, Amendment of Exclusion Law. (3428)
55th Congress, 1st session, 1897:
   Senate Document No. 120, Alleged Illegal Entry of Chinese. (3562)
   Senate Document No. 167, Alleged Illegal Entry of Chinese. (3563)
   House Document No. 68, Chinese for Omaha Exposition. (3571)
55th Congress, 2nd Session, 1897-1898:
   Senate Document No. 182, Amendment of Exclusion Law. (3600)
   House Report No. 1628, Amendment of Exclusion Law. (3722)
55th Congress, 3rd session, 1898-1899:
   Senate Report No. 1654, Extension of Immigration Laws to Hawaiian Islands. (3739)
56th Congress, 1st session, 1899-1900:
   House Document No. 1, Part 1, Foreign Relations, 1899. (3898)
56th Congress, 2nd session, 1900-1901:
   House Document No. 464, Extending the Time for Registration in Hawaii. (4163)
   House Documents Nos. 471 and 472, To Strengthen Exclusion Laws. (4163)
   House Report No. 2503, To Prevent Smuggling of Chinese. (4213)
57th Congress, 1st session, 1901-1902:
   Senate Document No. 106, Arguments against Exclusion. (4230)
   Senate Document No. 137, Some Reasons for Chinese Exclusion. (4231)
   Senate Documents Nos. 162 and 164, Wu Ting Fang on Chinese Exclusion. (4231)
   Senate Document No. 191, For the Re-enactment of the Chinese Exclusion Law; California Memorial. (4234)
   Senate Document No. 254, Chinese on American Vessels. (4235)
   Senate Document No. 281, Chinese on American Vessels. (4239)
   Senate Document No. 291, Laws, etc., Relating to Chinese Exclusion. (4239)
   Senate Document No. 292, Petition for Exclusion of Japanese and Chinese. (4239)
   Senate Document No. 300, Regulations Relating to Chinese Exclusion. (4239)
   Senate Document No. 304, Exclusion of Chinese Laborers. (4241)
   Senate Document No. 776, Chinese Exclusion: Hearings before Committee on Immigration. (4265)
   House Document No. 1, Foreign Relations, 1901. (4268)
   House Report No. 1231, Chinese Exclusion. (4403)
58th Congress, 3rd session, 1904-1905:
   House Document No. 1, Foreign Relations, 1904. (4780)
59th Congress, 1st session, 1905-1906:
   House Document No. 847, Enforcement of Chinese Exclusion Laws. (4990)

Compilations

DESTY, ROBERT (Editor), *The Federal Reporter: Cases Argued and Determined in the Circuit and District Courts of the United States.* Volumes 17, 18, 19, and 142. St. Paul, 1883-1884, 1906.

MALLOY, WILLIAM M. (Compiler), *Treaties, Conventions, International Acts, Protocols and Agreements between the United States and Other Powers, 1776-1909.* Senate Document No. 357, 61st Congress, 2nd session, 1910. 2 volumes.

MOORE, JOHN BASSETT (Compiler), *A Digest of International Law. House Document No. 551*, 56th Congress, 2nd session, 1901. 8 volumes.

RICHARDSON, JAMES D. (Compiler), *A Compilation of the Messages and Papers of the Presidents, 1789-1897.* Washington, 1900. 10 volumes.

SAWYER, L. S. B. (Reporter), *Reports of Cases Decided in the Circuit and District Courts of the United States for the Ninth Circuit.* San Francisco, 1873-1891. 14 volumes.

Statutes at Large of the United States of America. Volumes XVI, XVIII, XXII, XXIII, XXV, XXVII, XXVIII, XXX-XXXIII used, Boston, 1871; Washington, 1875-1905.

United States Immigration Commission (William P. Dillingham, Chairman), *Statistical Review of Immigration, 1820-1910. Senate Document No. 756,* 61st Congress, 3rd session, 1911. This is one of the forty-one volumes in the report of this commission.

United States Reports: Cases Adjudged in the Supreme Court of the United States. Volume 36 (11 Peters), Philadelphia, 1845. Volumes 48 (7 Howard) and 92 (2 Otto), Boston, 1849, 1876. Volume 78 (11 Wallace), Washington, 1871. Volumes 112 and 113 (1885), 118 (1886), 130 (1889), 149 (1893), and 163 (1896), New York, dates as given. Volume 194, New York, 1904.

The West Coast Reporter, Volume V. San Francisco, 1885.

WOLD, ANSEL (Compiler), *Biographical Directory of the American Congress, 1774-1927. House Document No. 783.* 69th Congress, 2nd session, 1928.

GOVERNMENT PUBLICATIONS: STATE

NOTE.—*The Journal of the Assembly,* the *Journal of the Senate,* and the Statutes of the various sessions of the legislature of the state of California were published by the State Printer during the year in which the session adjourned. The places of publication were: 1850 and 1851, San Jose; 1852, 1853, and 1854, San Francisco; and since 1855, Sacramento. The following have been used:

Journal of the Assembly, 1850, 1851, 1852, 1853, 1854, 1855, 1856, 1857, 1858, 1860, 1862, 1863, 1863-64, 1867-68, 1869-70, 1871-72, 1875-76, 1877-78, 1879-80, 1891, 1893.

Journal of the Senate, 1850, 1851, 1852, 1853, 1854, 1855, 1856, 1857, 1858, 1860, 1862, 1863, 1863-64, 1867-68, 1869-70, 1871-72, 1875-76, 1877-78, 1879-80, 1891, 1893.

Appendix to the Journal of the Assembly, 1855.

Appendix to the Legislative Journals, 1852, 1862, 1877-78, 1880, 1901.

Acts Amendatory to the Codes, 1873-74, 1877-78, 1880.

Code of Civil Procedure, 1872.

Statutes of the State of California, 1850, 1851, 1852, 1853, 1854, 1855, 1856, 1857, 1858, 1860, 1861, 1862, 1863, 1863-64, 1865-66, 1867-68, 1869-70, 1875-76, 1877-78, 1880, 1885.

Statutes and Amendments to the Codes, 1881, 1883-84, 1891, 1893, 1901.

Compilations

Bureau of Labor Statistics, *First Biennial Report, 1883-84* Sacramento, 1884.

————, *Fifth Biennial Report, 1891-1892.* Sacramento, 1893.

Debates and Proceedings of the Constitutional Convention of the State of California, Sacramento, Sept. 28, 1878-. Sacramento, 1881.

DEERING, F. P. (Compiler), *The Codes and Statutes of California.* San Francisco, 1885. 4 volumes.

GARFIELDE, S., and SNYDER, F. A. (Compilers), *Compiled Laws of the State of California.* Benicia, 1853.

HART, ALBERT (Compiler), *The Civil Code of the State of California.* San Francisco, 1876.

HITTELL, THEODORE H. (Compiler), *The General Laws of the State of California, from 1850 to 1864, Inclusive.* San Francisco, 1870.

————, *Supplement to the Codes and Statutes of the State of California.* San Francisco, 1880.

Reports of Cases Determined in the Supreme Court of the State of California. San Francisco, 1906. Volumes 1 (1850), 4 (1854), 7 (1857), 20 (1862), 36 (1868), 40 (1871), 42 (1872), 68 (1885), 101 (1894).

State Senate, *Chinese Immigration: Its Social, Moral, and Political Effect.* Report of the Special Committee on Chinese Immigration to the California State Senate. Sacramento, 1878.

TREADWELL, EDWARD T. (Annotator), *The Constitution of the State of California.* San Francisco: 1st edition, 1902; 5th edition, 1923.

MUNICIPAL PUBLICATIONS

Los Angeles City Council, *Municipal Reports, 1893.* Los Angeles, 1894.

San Francisco Board of Supervisors, *Municipal Reports,* 1859-60, 1865-66, 1869-70, 1871-72, 1874-75, 1875-76, 1876-77, 1878-79, 1884-85. San Francisco. Published in the respective years.

————, *General Orders,* 1871-72, 1888. San Francisco, same dates.

OBSERVATIONS, MEMOIRS, ETC.

BELL, HORACE, *On the Old West Coast.* New York, 1930. This is a reprint of an earlier edition.

BLAINE, JAMES G., *Twenty Years in Congress.* Norwich, 1884. 2 volumes.

BOWLES, SAMUEL, *Our New West.* Hartford, 1869.

BRACE, CHARLES L., *The New West.* New York, 1869. In the two foregoing works the authors were reporting on their travels in California.

COLE, CORNELIUS, *Memoirs of.* New York, 1908. Cole served as congressman and senator from California during and after the Civil War.

CONDIT, IRA M., *The Chinaman As We See Him, and Fifty Years of Work for Him.* New York, 1900. Mr. Condit had been a Presbyterian missionary among the Chinese on the Pacific coast for almost thirty years prior to writing this book.

CONE, MARY, *Two Years in California.* Chicago, 1876.

DOONER, P. W., *Last Days of the Republic.* San Francisco, 1880. An imaginary "history" of the gradual occupation and conquest of the United States by the Chinese during the last two decades of the nineteenth century.

GIBSON, O(TIS), *The Chinese in America.* Cincinnati, 1877. Mr. Gibson had been a missionary in China and was in charge of the Methodist mission for the Chinese on the coast.

HITTELL, J. S., *History of San Francisco.* San Francisco, 1878.

NEWMARK, HARRIS, *Sixty Years in Southern California.* Chicago, 1925.

SEWARD, GEORGE F., *Chinese Immigration, in Its Social and Economical Aspects.* New York, 1881. Seward was United States minister to China, 1877-1880, and prior to that consul-general at Shanghai. Strongly pro-Chinese.

SPEER, WILLIAM, *The Oldest and the Newest Empire, or China and the United States.* Hartford, 1870. Speer, a Presbyterian minister, organized the first mission among the Chinese on the coast in 1853.

TUTHILL, FRANKLIN, *The History of California.* San Francisco, 1866.

PAMPHLETS

NOTE.—Horace Davis, while a member of Congress 1877-1881, and afterward, collected pamphlets which are now bound in four volumes and deposited in Bancroft Library at Berkeley. Some of the following are from this collection and are so indicated.

American Federation of Labor, *Some Reasons for Exclusion.* Washington, 1902.

Anti-Chinese Union, *Constitution and By-Laws of the Anti-Chinese Union of San Francisco.* San Francisco, 1876. Davis, IV.

ARCHIBALD, JOHN, *On the Contact of Races* (California Miscellany, Vol. I, No. 4). San Francisco, 1860. Combats the idea of destructive competition with white labor and advocates citizenship for the Chinese.

BAKER, EDWARD P., *The Chinese Question.* San Francisco, 1878. Davis, III.

BECKER, SAMUEL E. W., *Humors of a Congressional Investigating Committee.* Washington, 1877. Davis, II. This is a criticism of the report of the Congressional Committee of 1876, by a Roman Catholic.

BEE, F. A. *Opening Argument before the Join Committee of the Two Houses of Congress on Chinese Immigration.* San Francisco, 1876. Davis, III. Also in *Report 689,* 34-50.

BENNETT, H. C., *Chinese Labor.* San Francisco, 1870. Davis, I. A lecture before the San Francisco Mechanics' Institute. Pro-Chinese.

BLAKESLEE, S. V., *Address on Chinese Immigration.* No date. No publisher. Davis, I. Also in California Senate, *Chinese Immigration.* This address was given before the General Association of Congregational Churches of California at Sacramento, October, 1877, and marked the first serious break in the attitude of the Churches toward the Chinese.

BOALT, JOHN H., *The Chinese Question.* No date. A paper read before the Berkeley Club, August, 1877. Reprinted in California Senate, *Chinese Immigration,* 253-262.

BROOKS, BENJAMIN S. (Compiler), *Brief of the Legislation and Adjudication Touching the Chinese Question.* San Francisco, 1877.

————, *Opening Statement before the Joint Committee of the two Houses of Congress on Chinese Immigration.* San Francisco, 1876. Includes J. A. Whitney, *The Chinese and the Chinese Question,* and Samuel Wells Williams, *Our Relations with the Chinese Empire.*

————, *Appendix to the Opening Statement and Brief of B. S. Brooks on the Chinese Question.* San Francisco, 1877. Davis, II.

CAPP, CHARLES S., *The Church and Chinese Immigration.* San Francisco, 1890. Davis, III.

CLAYTON, J. E., *On the Chinese Question.* Speech delivered in 1855. Davis, I.

CONDIT, Mrs. I. M., *Chinese in America.* Questions and answers for Mission Circles and Bands. Philadelphia. No date, but after 1882. Davis, III.

COWDIN, ELLIOT C., *Chinese Immigration: Maintain the National Faith.* Speech delivered February 27, 1879.

CULIN, STEWART, *China in America.* Philadelphia, 1887. Davis, I.

DENSMORE, G. B., *The Chinese in California.* San Francisco, 1880. ". . . . designed mainly for circulation east of the Rocky Mountains."

FARWELL, W. B., *The Chinese at Home and Abroad.* With Report of the Special Committee of the Board of Supervisors of San Francisco on the condition of the Chinese quarters of that city. San Francosco, 1885.

FIELD, STEPHEN J., *Power of the State to Exclude Foreigners.* Opinion in the case of Ah Fong, in the United States Circuit Court for the District of California, September 21, 1874. San Francisco, 1874. Davis, III.

Friends of International Right and Justice, *How the U. S. Treaty with China is Observed in California.* With an appendix: "Widespread conspiracy to drive the Chinese out of the State." San Francisco, 1877. Davis, I.

GIBSON, O., *Chinaman or White Man, Which?* San Francisco, 1873. Davis, III. A reply to Father Burchard's address on the same subject.

————, Letter to Horace Davis, April 2, 1880. Davis, II.

GRIMM, HENRY, *The Chinese Must Go.* San Francisco, 1879.

HEALY, PATRICK JOSEPH, *A Shoemaker's Contribution to the Chinese Discussion.* No date. Davis, III.

————, *Reasons for Non-Exclusion.* San Francisco, 1902. Very largely a criticism of the anti-Chinese convention, Nov., 1901.

HEALY, PATRICK JOSEPH, and NG POON CHEW, *A Statement for Non-Exclusion.* San Francisco, 1905. A rather detailed history of the Chinese question in California from the beginning.

HOPKINS, C. T., *Common Sense Applied to the Immigration Question.* 1869.

IOTA (F. GATES), *The Raid of the Dragons into Eagle-land.* San Francisco, 1878. An allegorical presentation of the state Senate investigation report. Davis, III.

KERR, J. G., *The Chinese Question Analyzed.* San Francisco, 1877. Dr. Kerr was for twenty-three years a resident of China. Davis, I.

LAI CHUN CHUEN, *Remarks of the Chinese Merchants of San Francisco upon Governor Bigler's Message.* San Francisco, 1855. Davis, I.

LAYRES, AUGUSTUS, *Both Sides of the Chinese Question.* San Francisco, 1887. Davis, I.

——————, *The Other Side of the Chinese Question.* San Francisco, 1886. Davis, I.

LOBSCHEID, W., *The Chinese: What They Are and What They Are Doing.* San Francisco, 1873. Davis, I.

MCALLISTER, WILLIAM F., *Immigration Report, 1887.* San Francisco, 1887. Davis, IV.

MEADE, EDWIN R., *The Chinese Question.* New York, 1877. Davis, II. Also printed in California Senate, *Chinese Immigration.*

MEIN, CHARLES STUART, *Speeches on the Chinese Question.* Delivered in the Legislative Council of Queensland, July 4 and 11, 1877. (Reprinted from Hansard). Davis, II.

Pro-Chinese Minority, *To the American People, President and Congress.* Dec. 26, 1879. A broadside in reply to Gov. Irwin's circular on the state vote against the Chinese. Davis, I.

Representative Assembly of Trades and Labor Unions of the Pacific Coast, *An Appeal from the Pacific Coast to the Workingmen and Women of the United States.* 1881. Davis, III. Statistics on labor and the Chinese in California.

Republican State Central Committee, *Petition to President Arthur on the Chinese Question.* 1882. Davis, II.

ROBERTS, W. K., *The Mongolian Problem in America.* San Francisco, 1906.

RYER, WASHINGTON M., *The Conflict of the Races.* San Francisco, 1886. Davis, IV.

SAWYER, LORENZO, and HOFFMAN, OGDEN, *Rights of Chinese.* Decision in the United States Circuit Court in the case of Tiburcio Parrott. March 22, 1880. Davis, II.

Six Chinese Companies, *Memorial of the Six Chinese Companies: The Testimony of California's Leading Citizens before the Joint Special Congressional Committee.* San Francisco, 1877. Davis, I.

SPEER, WILLIAM, *An Humble Plea.* Addressed to the Legislature of California in Behalf of the Immigrants from the Empire of China to this State. San Francisco, 1856. Davis, IV. Speer was the Presbyterian missionary among the Chinese.

——————, *China and California: Their Relations Past and Present.* San Francisco, 1853. Davis, IV.

STARR, M. B., *The Coming Struggle; or What the People of the Pacific Coast Think of the Coolie Invasion.* San Francisco, 1873. Largely a collection of newspaper articles.

SWINTON, JOHN, *The Chinese-American Question.* New York, 1870. First published in the New York *Tribune*, June 30, 1870.

TOWNSEND, L. T., *The Chinese Problem.* Boston, 1876. This was an influential pro-Chinese pamphlet.

United Brothers of California, *Constitution and By-Laws of the United Brothers of California.* San Francisco, 1876. Davis, IV. A radical anti-coolie organization.

WEST, HENRY J. (Compiler), *The Chinese Invasion.* San Francisco, 1873. A compilation of newspaper articles and editorials on the Chinese, including that of Henry George as printed in the New York *Tribune*, May 1, 1869.

WHITNEY, JAMES A., *The Chinese and the Chinese Question.* New York, 1880. Davis, I.

WILLIAMS, S. WELLS, *Chinese Immigration.* New York, 1879. Davis, II.

————, *Our Relations with the Chinese Empire.* San Francisco, 1877. Davis, I.

WOLTER, ROBERT, *A Short and Truthful History of the Taking of California and Oregon by the Chinese, in the year A.D. 1899.* San Francisco, 1882. An imaginary "history" by a "survivor," in the vein of Flóyd Gibbons' *The Red Napoleon.*

Workingmen's Party of California, *Chinatown Declared a Nuisance!* San Francisco, 1880.

ANONYMOUS, *Address from the Workingmen of San Francisco to their Brothers throughout the Pacific Coast. Adopted in mass meeting,* August 16, 1888. Davis, I.

————, *Proceedings of California Chinese Exclusion Convention.* San Francisco, November 21, 22, 1901. San Francisco, 1901.

————, *The Invalidity of the "Queue Ordinance" of the City and County of San Francisco. (Ho Ah Kow v. Matthew Nunan).* San Francisco, 1879. An appendix contains a history of anti-Chinese legislation.

————, *Truth v. Fiction, Justice v. Prejudice. A plain and unvarnished statement why Exclusion Laws against the Chinese should NOT be Re-enacted.* No date. An answer to *Some Reasons for Exclusion,* issued by the American Federation of Labor, 1902.

————, *Uncle Sam-ee and His Little Chi-nee.* New York, 1879. Davis, II.

NEWSPAPERS AND PERIODICALS

NOTE.—All San Francisco newspapers are cited in the footnotes without the name of the city, but all other newspapers have the name of their respective cities included.

Newspapers most frequently quoted

Sacramento *Record-Union,* 1871- . For about five years before this there were two papers, uniting to make the *Record-Union.*

San Francisco *Daily Alta California* (quoted simply as *Alta*), 1850-1891. For many years the most ably edited paper on the coast. Conservative, and only occasionally anti-Chinese. Ceased publication June 2, 1891.

San Francisco *Evening Bulletin,* 1855-   Founded by James King of William. Anti-Chinese from later sixties on. Fremont Older became its editor in the late nineties.

San Francisco *Morning Call,* 1856-   Owned and managed by very much the same group which published the *Bulletin.* Anti-Chinese after the late sixties.

San Francisco *Chronicle,* 1865- . Founded and edited by Charles and M. H. De Young. Generally anti-Chinese, but fluctuating with political conditions.

San Francisco *Evening Post,* 1865-   Strongly anti-Chinese, and the self-styled champion of the Workingmen's Party. Henry George was one of its early editors.

NOTE.—The following newspapers have been used occasionally, most of the editorials having been secured through *Bancroft Scraps,* Vols. VI-IX, *Chinese,* Bancroft Library, University of California:

Alameda *Independent,* March 25, 1876.
Argonaut, Oct. 27, Nov. 3, 10, 17, Dec. 1, 29, 1877; Jan. 26, 1878; Dec. 26, 1885.
Auburn *Placer Herald,* June 5, 1875.
Boise City (Idaho) *Statesman,* Aug. 28, 1869.
Boston *Advertiser,* June 29, 1869.
Boston *Journal,* Dec. 12, 1868.
Butte *Record,* July 1, 1876.

California Independent, March 20, 1880.
Chicago *Inter-Ocean,* Dec. 25, 1877.
Chicago *Tribune,* Aug. 16, 1869; June 11, 1870.
Cincinnati *Commercial,* Sept. 13, 1869; July 12, 1870.
Eureka *West Coast Signal,* Jan. 6, 1875.
Grass Valley *National,* June 15, 16, 17, 26, 1869.
London *Telegraph,* Nov. 28, 1877.
Humboldt Register (Unionville, Nevada), April 24, 29, 1869.
Los Angeles *Examiner,* March 4, 8, 27, 1880.
Los Angeles *Express,* July 30, Oct. 21, 30, 31, 1879; Jan. 5, 23, 29, Feb. 14, 16, 19, 1880.
Los Angeles *Herald,* Jan. 23, May 31, 1881.
Los Angeles *News,* July 17, Dec. 11, 1861; July 10, 1866; Feb. 17, March 17, July 1, 6, 7, Aug. 5, 7, 20, 22, 24, Oct. 19, Dec. 4, 1869; March 11, 1871.
Los Angeles *Star,* March 17, May 5, 1860; Feb. 8, 1862; Oct. 25, 26, 1871; Oct. 8, 1875; March 1, 17, 1877.
Marin Journal, March 30, April 13, 1876.
Marysville *Appeal,* March 18, 1862; Dec. 25, 1868; Jan. 17, 1869.
Mendocino *Democrat,* March 25, April 8, 1876.
Monterey *Democrat,* April 17, 1869.
Nevada *Transcript,* Dec. 6, 1867; Oct. 3, Nov. 17, 20, 1876.
New Orleans *Times,* Aug. 26, 1868.
New York *Herald,* Oct. 3, 1868.
New York *Independent,* Aug. 19, Oct. 28, 1869.
New York *Times,* Dec. 22, 1877.
New York *Tribune,* July 28, 1869; June 15, 1872; April 3, 1880.
New York *World,* May 15, 1877.
Petaluma *Argus,* Oct. 9, 1874.
Oakland *Transcript,* March 19, 29, 31, April 4, 6, 14, Oct. 15, Nov. 15, 1876.
Occident, August 26, Nov. 22, 1867.
Oneida (N. Y.) *Dispatch,* June 24, 1870.
Pacific, Jan. 9, 16, Feb. 5, March 12, 26, Aug. 13, 27, Sept. 10, 1879.
Philadelphia *Press,* July 10, 1868.
Placerville *Union,* June 17, 1869.
Sacramento *Bee,* April 4, 5, 6, 12, May 4, 23, 29, June 28, Oct. 16, Nov. 18, 1876.
St. Louis *Democrat,* Sept. 9, 1869; July 12, 1870.
San Diego *Union,* July 6, 1876.
San Francisco *Critic,* May 1, 1868.
San Francisco *Examiner,* July 9, 1870; June 5, 1875; Feb. 14, March 13, 1880; Oct. 23, 1888; Jan. 4, 5, 6, 8, 23, 1889.
San Francisco *Express,* March 7, 1867.
San Francisco *Herald,* May 15, 1869.
San Francisco *New Letter,* April 1, 1876.
San Francisco *Picayune,* Sept. 16, 1851.
San Francisco *Record,* July 4, 1868.
San Francisco *Sentinel,* March 30, 1867.
San Francisco *Times,* Aug. 7, 1867; June 26, July 16, 1869.
San Francisco *Tribune,* Dec. 24, 1869.
Santa Cruz *Courier,* Nov. 24, 1876.
Santa Cruz *Independent,* April 15, 1876.
Sonoma *Democrat,* March 25, April 8, 1876.
Sonora *Flag,* Feb. 19, 1863.
Stockton *Independent,* March 24, April 10, 12, May 15, 17, 18, 19, 24, July 24, August 18, Oct. 23, Dec. 29, 1876.
Unitarian Outlook, April, 1879.
Yolo *Democrat,* March 23, April 28, May 25, June 1, 8, 22, 1876.
Yreka *Union,* July 5, 1876.

Magazine Articles

BACON, THOMAS R., "The Railroad Strike in California," *Yale Review*, III, 241-250, November, 1894.
DE VARIGNY, M. C., "L'Invasion Chinoise et Le Socialisme aux Etats-Unis," *Revue de Deux Mondes*, XXIX, 589-613, Oct. 1, 1878. Davis, II.
GEORGE, HENRY, "The Kearney Agitation in California," *Popular Science Monthly*, XVII, 433, August, 1880.
GOODENOUGH, S., "Foes of Labor," *California Review*, I, 34-40, October, 1893.
Ho Yow, "Chinese Exclusion: A Benefit or a Harm," *North American Review*, CLXXIII, 314-330, September, 1901. Ho Yow was Chinese consul-general in the United States.
MAGEE, THOMAS, "China's Menace to the World," *Forum*, X, 197-206, October, 1890. Davis, IV.
MANSFIELD, EDWIN D., "The Chinese Question in the United States," *The International Review*, III, 833-841, November-December, 1876. Davis, II.
MEDHURST, SIR WALTER, "The Chinese as Colonists," *The Nineteenth Century*, September, 1878, pp. 517-527. Davis, II.
"Memoirs of Lemuel Clarke McKeeby," *California Historical Society Quarterly*, III, 45-72, April, 1924.
MILLER, JOHN F., "Certain Phases of the Chinese Question," *The Californian*, I, 237-242, March, 1880.
PHELAN, JAMES D., "Why the Chinese Should Be Excluded," *North American Review*, CLXXIII, 663-676, November, 1901.
(Unsigned), "The Chinese," *Hutching's California Magazine*, IV, 535-537, June, 1860.
(Unsigned), "The Chinese Six Companies," "How Our Chinese Are Employed," "Chinese Women in California," "National Characteristics," "The Chinese Labor Problems," and "The Commerce of Asia and Oceania," *Overland Monthly*, I, 221-227, II, 231-240, 344-351, III, 253-257, 407-419, VIII, 171-175. Bret Harte was editor of the *Overland Monthly* during the period 1868-1871 and probably wrote these articles.
UTTER, DAVID N., "The Chinese Must Go," *The Unitarian Review*, XII, 48-56, July, 1879. Davis, II.
YAN PHOU LEE, "The Chinese Must Stay," *North American Review*, CXLVIII, 476-483, April, 1889. Davis, IV.

GENERAL ACCOUNTS, COLLECTIONS, AND MONOGRAPHS

ABBOTT, EDITH, *Historical Aspects of the Immigration Problem. Select Documents.* Chicago, 1926.
American Relations with China: A report of the Conference held at Johns Hopkins University, September 17-20, 1925. Baltimore, 1925. Contains bibliography on present day conditions.
BANCROFT, HUBERT HOWE, *History of California* (*Works*, XVIII-XXIV). San Francisco, 1884-1890. 7 volumes.
————, *California Inter Pocula* (*Works*, XXXV). San Francisco, 1888.
————, *Popular Tribunals* (*Works*, XXXVI-XXXVII). San Francisco, 1887. 2 volumes.
————, *Nevada, Colorado and Wyoming* (*Works*, XXV). San Francisco, 1890.
BEARD, CHARLES A., and MARY R., *The Rise of American Civilization.* New York, 1930.
BEMIS, SAMUEL FLAGG (Editor), *The American Secretaries of State and Their Diplomacy.* New York, 1927-1929. 10 volumes.
BODE, WILLIAM WALTER, *Lights and Shadows of Chinatown.* San Francisco, 1896.
BRYCE, JAMES, *The American Commonwealth.* London and New York, 1891. 2 volumes.
CAMPBELL, PERSIA CRAWFORD, *Chinese Coolie Emigration to Countries within the British Empire.* London, 1923.

CLELAND, ROBERT GLASS, *A History of California: The American Period.* New York, 1922.

CLELAND, ROBERT GLASS, and HARDY, OSGOOD, *March of Industry.* Los Angeles, 1929. This is one of the series of books on the history of California edited by John Russell McCarthy.

COMMONS, JOHN R., *Races and Immigrants in America.* New York, 1920.

COMMONS, JOHN R., et al., *History of Labour in the United States.* New York, 1918. 2 volumes.

COOK, ARTHUR E., and HAGERTY, JOHN J., *Immigration Laws of the United States, Compiled and Explained.* Chicago, 1929.

COOLIDGE, MARY ROBERTS, *Chinese Immigration.* New York, 1909. The best work on the subject.

COY, OWEN C., *The Genesis of California Counties.* Berkeley, 1923.

————, *Gold Days,* Los Angeles, 1929. One of the series edited by John Russell McCarthy.

COY, OWEN C., and JONES, HERBERT C., *California's Constitution.* Los Angeles, 1930.

CUMMINS, ELLA STEARNS, *The Story of the Files.* San Francisco, 1893.

DAGGETT, STUART, *Chapters on the History of the Southern Pacific.* New York, 1922.

DIXON, WILLIAM HEPWORTH, *White Conquest.* London, 1876. 2 volumes. The discussion of the Chinese in California, in volume II, is anti-Chinese and not too careful as to facts.

EAVES, LUCILE, *A History of California Labor Legislation,* with an introductory sketch of the San Francisco labor movement. Berkeley, 1910.

ELDREDGE, ZOETH SKINNER (Editor) *History of California.* New York, 1915. 5 volumes. The first three volumes and half of the fourth were written by Clinton A. Snowden.

ELLISON, JOSEPH, *California and the Nation, 1850-1869.* Berkeley, 1927.

FAIRCHILD, HENRY PRATT, *Immigration: A World Movement and Its American Significance.* New York, 1923.

FANKHAUSER, WILLIAM C., *A Financial History of California: Public Revenues, Debts, and Expenditures (University of California Publications in Economics, Volume 3, No. 2).* Berkeley, 1913.

FOSTER, JOHN W., *American Diplomacy in the Orient.* Boston, 1903.

GARIS, ROY L., *Immigration Restriction: A Study of the Opposition to and Regulation of Immigration into the United States.* New York, 1927.

GARNER, JAMES W., *American Foreign Policies:* An examination and evaluation of certain traditional and recent international policies of the United States. New York, 1928.

HITTELL, THEODORE H., *History of California.* San Francisco, 1898.

HUNT, ROCKWELL D., *California and Californians.* Chicago, 1926.

HUNT, ROCKWELL D., and AMENT, WILLIAM SHEFFIELD, *Oxcart to Airplane.* Los Angeles, 1929. One of the series edited by John Russell McCarthy.

JENKS, JEREMIAH W., LAUCK, W. JETT, and SMITH, RUFUS D., *The Immigration Problem.* A study of American immigration conditions and needs. New York, 1926. 6th edition. Based upon the findings of the Immigration Commission.

McKENZIE, RODERICK D., *Oriental Exclusion: The effect of American immigration laws, regulations and judicial decisions upon the Chinese and Japanese on the American Pacific Coast.* New York, 1927.

McMASTER, JOHN BACH, *A History of the People of the United States, from the Revolution to the Civil War.* New York, 1883-1913. 8 volumes.

MAYO-SMITH, RICHMOND, *Emigration and Immigration.* New York, 1890.

MEARS, ELIOT GRINNELL, *Resident Orientals on the American Pacific Coast: Their Legal and Economic Status.* New York, 1927.

MORSE, HOSEA BALLOU, *The International Relations of the Chinese Empire.* London, 1910, 1918. 3 volumes.

————, *The Trade and Administration of the Chinese Empire.* London, 1908. A very excellent chart of the trade of China, 1864-1904, is on page 270.

Norton, Henry K., *The Story of California.* Chicago, 1925.
Rhodes, James Ford, *History of the United States from the Compromise of 1850 to the McKinley-Bryan Campaign of 1896.* New York, 1920. 8 volumes.
Schlesinger, Arthur Meier, *Political and Social History of the United States, 1829-1925.* New York, 1928.
Sparks, Edwin Erle, *National Development, 1877-1885 (The American Nation: A History,* Albert Bushnell Hart, Editor. Vol. XXIII). New York, 1907.
Stanwood, Edward, *A History of the Presidency.* 2 volumes. Boston, 1916, 1924.
Stewart, Bryce M., *Canadian Labor Laws and the Treaty.* New York, 1926.
Swisher, Carl Brent, *Motivation and Political Technique in the California Constitutional Convention, 1878-1879.* Claremont, 1930.
Ta Chen, *Chinese Migrations.* Bulletin of the Bureau of Labor Statistics No. 340. Washington, 1923. Contains a selected bibliography.
Thornbury, D. L., *California's Redwood Wonderland: Humboldt County.* San Francisco, 1923.
Tien-lu Li, *Congressional Policy of Chinese Immigration; or Legislation Relating to Chinese Immigration to the United States.* Nashville, 1916. Contains a good bibliography on this phase of the subject.
Treat, Payson J., *The Far East: A Political and Diplomatic History.* New York, 1928.
Tyler, Alice Felt, *The Foreign Policy of James G. Blaine.* Minneapolis, 1927.
Wicher, Edward Arthur, *The Presbyterian Church in California, 1849-1927.* New York, 1927.
Williams, Edward T., *China: Yesterday and Today.* New York, 1929.
Williams, Frederick Wells, *Anson Burlingame and the First Chinese Mission to Foreign Powers.* New York, 1912.
Williams, Mary Floyd, *History of the San Francisco Committee of Vigilance of 1851.* Berkeley, 1921.
Williams, S. Wells, *The Middle Kingdom. A Survey of the Geography, Government, Literature, Social Life, Arts and History of the Chinese Empire.* Revised edition. 2 volumes. New York, 1913.

REVIEW ARTICLES

Ching Chao Wu, *Chinatowns: A Study in Symbiosis and Assimilation.* In University of Chicago, *Abstracts of Theses,* Humanistic Series, VII, 351-354. Chicago, 1930.
Cole, Arthur C., "Nativism in the Lower Mississippi Valley," *Proceedings of the Mississippi Valley Historical Association,* 1912-13, VI, 258-275.
Dennett, Tyler, "Seward's Far Eastern Policy," *American Historical Review,* XXVIII, 45-62, October, 1922.
Dorland, C. P., "Chinese Massacre at Los Angeles in 1871," *Annual Publications, Historical Society of Southern California,* Vol. III, Part II, pp. 22-26. Los Angeles, 1894.
Dunning, William A., "Truth in History," *American Historical Review,* XIX, 217-229, January, 1914.
Hansen, Marcus L., "The History of American Immigration as a Field for Research," *American Historical Review,* XXXII, 500-518, April, 1927.
Pyau Ling, "Causes of Chinese Emigration," *Annals of the American Academy of Political and Social Science,* XXXIX, 74-82, January, 1912.
Stephenson, George M., "Nativism in the Forties and Fifties, with Special Reference to the Mississippi Valley," *Mississippi Valley Historical Review,* IX, 185-202, December, 1922.
Wellborn, Mildred, "Events Leading to the Chinese Exclusion Acts," *Annual Publications, Historical Society of Southern California,* IX, 49-58.
Wheaton, Donald W., "Spotlights on the Political History of California from 1887 to 1898," *California Historical Society Quarterly,* V, 282-288, September, 1926.

SUPPLEMENTARY BIBLIOGRAPHY, 1939–72

GIVEN the current interest in and urgency of ethnic studies in the United States, one can expect a further burgeoning of Asian American studies in general and Chinese American studies in particular. We very much need a history of Chinese Americans; before we get that kind of synthesis, there should be a variety of local and regional studies. We know virtually nothing, for example, about the history and development of the Chinese community in San Francisco, not to mention those in other metropolitan centers. For a variety of reasons, including a lack of primary sources and the language barrier, most of the best work has focused on the oppressors rather than the oppressed. One exception to this generalization is James W. Loewen, *The Mississippi Chinese* (1971), which probes analytically the micro-community of Chinese in the Mississippi delta but from which few generalizations about the major Chinese American communities may be drawn. The bibliography which follows, while far from complete, lists most of the historical writing that bears directly on Chinese American studies published since 1939.

ROGER DANIELS

Armstrong, W. M. "Godkin and Chinese Labor: A Paradox in Nineteenth Century Liberalism." *American Journal of Economics and Sociology,* 21 (Jan., 1962): 91-102.

Barth, Gunther. *Bitter Strength: A History of the Chinese in the United States, 1850-1870.* Cambridge, Mass.: Harvard University Press, 1964.

Black, Isabella. "American Labour and Chinese Immigration." *Past and Present,* 25 (July, 1963): 59-76.

Caldwell, Dan. "The Negroization of the Chinese Stereotype in California." *Southern California Quarterly,* 53 (Mar., 1971): 123-135.

California, Department of Industrial Relations, Division of Fair Employment Practices. *Californians of Japanese, Chinese, Filipino Ancestry: Population; Employment; Income; Education.* San Francisco, 1965.

Carranco, Lynwood. "Chinese Expulsion from Humboldt County." *Pacific Historical Review,* 30 (Nov., 1961): 329-340.

Chiu, Ping. *Chinese Labor in California, 1850-1880: An Economic Study.* Madison: State Historical Society of Wisconsin, 1963.

Choy, Philip P. "Golden Mountain of Lead: The Chinese Experience in California." *California Historical Quarterly,* 50 (Sept., 1970): 267-276.

Chu, George. "Chinatowns in the Delta: The Chinese in the Sacramento–San Joaquin Delta, 1876-1960." *California Historical Quarterly,* 50 (Mar., 1970): 277-286.

Crane, Paul, and Alfred Larson. "The Chinese Massacre." *Annals of Wyoming,* 12 (Jan., Apr., 1940): 47-55, 153-160.

Curti, Merle, and John Stalker. " 'The Flowery Flag Devils' — The American Image in China, 1840-1900." *Proceedings of the American Philosophical Society,* 96 (Dec., 1952): 663-690.

Daniels, Roger. *The Politics of Prejudice: The Anti-Japanese Movement in California and the Struggle for Japanese Exclusion.* Berkeley and Los Angeles: University of California Press, 1962.

———. "Westerners from the East: Oriental Immigrants Reappraised." *Pacific Historical Review,* 35 (Nov., 1966): 373-383.

———, and H. L. Kitano. *American Racism: Exploration of the Nature of Prejudice.* Englewood Cliffs, N.J.: Prentice-Hall, 1970.

———, and Eric F. Petersen. "California's Grandfather Clause: The Literacy in English Amendment of 1894." *Southern California Quarterly,* 50 (Mar., 1968): 51-56.

Divine, Robert A. *American Immigration Policy, 1924-1952.* New Haven, Conn.: Yale University Press, 1952.

Dulles, Foster R. *China and America: The Story of Their Relations since 1784.* Princeton, N.J.: Princeton University Press, 1946.

Fairbank, John K. *The United States and China.* Cambridge, Mass.: Harvard University Press, 1948.

Fuller, Varden L. *The Supply of Agricultural Labor as a Factor in the Evolution of Farm Organization in California,* Part 54 of *Hearings before a Subcommittee of the Committee on Education and Labor, United States Senate, 76th Congress, 3rd Session, pursuant to S. Res. 266 (74th Congress).* Washington, 1940.

Higham, John. *Strangers in the Land: Patterns of American Nativism, 1860-1925.* New Brunswick, N.J.: Rutgers University Press, 1955.

Hoy, William. *The Chinese Six Companies.* San Francisco: privately printed, 1942.

Hsu, Francis L. K. *Americans and Chinese: Two Ways of Life.* New York: Schuman, 1953.

————. *The Challenge of the American Dream: The Chinese in the United States.* Belmont, Calif.: Wadsworth, 1971.

Hyde, Stuart W. "The Chinese Stereotype in American Melodrama." *California Historical Society Quarterly,* 34 (Dec., 1955): 357-368.

Isaacs, Harold. *Scratches on Our Mind: American Images of China and India.* New York: John Day, 1958.

Jones, Dorothy B. *The Portrayal of China and India on the American Screen, 1896-1955.* Cambridge, Mass.: Harvard University Press, 1955.

Karlin, Jules A. "The Anti-Chinese Outbreaks in Seattle." *Pacific Northwest Quarterly,* 39 (Apr., 1948): 103-130.

Kauer, Ralph. "The Workingmen's Party of California." *Pacific Historical Review,* 13 (Sept., 1944): 278-291.

Kung, S. W. *The Chinese in American Life: Some Aspects of Their History, Status, Problems and Contributions.* Seattle: University of Washington Press, 1962.

Lee, Calvin. *Chinatown, U.S.A.* New York: Doubleday, 1965.

Lee, Rose Hum. *The Chinese in the United States of America.* Hong Kong: Hong Kong University Press, 1960.

Liu, Kwang Ching. *Americans and Chinese.* Cambridge, Mass.: Harvard University Press, 1963.

Locklear, William R. "The Celestials and the Angels." *Southern California Quarterly,* 42 (Sept., 1960): 239-254.

Loewen, James W. *The Mississippi Chinese: Between Black and White.* Cambridge, Mass.: Harvard University Press, 1971.

Lum, William Wong, comp. *Asians in America: A Bibliography of Master's Theses and Doctoral Dissertations.* Asian American Research Project, University of California, Davis, 1970.

Lyman, Stanford M. *The Asian in the West.* Reno and Las Vegas, Nev.: Desert Research Institute, 1970.

————. "The Structure of Chinese Society in Nineteenth Century America." Unpublished Ph.D. dissertation, University of California, Berkeley, 1961.

McClellan, Robert. *The Heathen Chinee: A Study of American Attitudes toward China, 1890-1905.* Columbus: Ohio State University Press, 1971.

McGloin, John B. *Eloquent Indian: The Life of James Bouchard, California Jesuit.* Stanford, Calif.: Stanford University Press, 1949.

————. "Thomas Ciao, Pioneer Chinese Priest in California." *California Historical Society Quarterly,* 48 (Mar., 1969): 45-58.

McWilliams, Carey. *Factories in the Field.* Boston: Little, Brown, 1939.

Mann, Arthur. "Gompers and the Irony of Racism." *Antioch Review,* 13 (June, 1953): 203-214.

Miller, Stuart Creighton. *The Unwelcome Immigrant: The American Image of the Chinese, 1785-1882.* Berkeley and Los Angeles: University of California Press, 1969.

Moon, Robert W. "The Contribution of Minority Races to California History." *Proceedings of the Second Conference of California Historical Societies,* 1956.

Morley, Charles. "The Chinese in California as Reported by Henry Sienkiewicz." *California Historical Society Quarterly,* 34 (Dec., 1955): 301-316.

North, Hart H. "Chinese and Japanese Immigration to the Pacific Coast." *California Historical Society Quarterly,* 28 (Dec., 1949): 343-350.

———. "Chinese Highbinder Societies in California." *California Historical Society Quarterly,* 23 (Dec., 1944): 335-347.

Olmstead, Roger. "The Chinese Must GO!" *California Historical Quarterly,* 50 (Sept., 1970): 285-294.

Paul, Rodman W. "The Origin of the Chinese Issue in California." *Mississippi Valley Historical Review,* 25 (Sept., 1938): 181-196.

Pitt, Leonard. "The Beginnings of Nativism in California." *Pacific Historical Review,* 30 (Feb., 1961): 23-38.

Ridout, Lionel U. "The Church, the Chinese and the Negroes in California." *Historical Magazine of the Protestant Episcopal Church,* 29 (Mar., 1959): 28-42.

Riggs, Fred. *Pressures on Congress.* New York: King's Crown, 1950.

Rodecape, Lois. "Celestial Drama in the Golden Hills: The Chinese Theater in California, 1849-1869." *California Historical Society Quarterly,* 23 (June, 1944): 97-116.

Rowland, Donald. "The United States and the Contract Labor Question in Hawaii, 1862-1900." *Pacific Historical Review,* 2 (Aug., 1933): 249-269.

Rudolph, Frederick. "Chinamen in Yankeedom: Anti-Unionism in Massachusetts in 1870." *American Historical Review,* 53 (Oct., 1947): 1-29.

Saxton, Alexander. "The Army of Canton in the High Sierra." *Pacific Historical Review,* 35 (May, 1966): 141-152.

———. *The Indispensable Enemy: Labor and the Anti-Chinese Movement in California.* Berkeley and Los Angeles: University of California Press, 1971.

———. "Race in the House of Labor." In Gary Nash and Richard Weiss, eds., *Race in the Mind of America.* New York: Holt, Rinehart and Winston, 1970.

Seager, Robert. "Some Denominational Reactions to Chinese Immigration to California, 1856-1892." *Pacific Historical Review,* 28 (Feb., 1959): 49-66.

Somma, Nicholas A. "The Knights of Labor and Chinese Immigration." Unpublished M.A. thesis, Catholic University, 1952.

Sung, Betty Lee. *Mountain of Gold.* New York: Macmillan, 1967; paperback (*The Story of the Chinese in America*), New York: Collier Books, 1971.

Thompson, Richard A. "The Yellow Peril, 1890-1925." Unpublished Ph.D. dissertation, University of Wisconsin, 1958.

Varg, Paul A. *The Making of a Myth: The United States and China, 1879-1912.* East Lansing: Michigan State University Press, 1968.

———. *Missionaries, Chinese and Diplomats.* Princeton, N.J.: Princeton University Press, 1958.

Walsh, Henry L. *Hallowed Were the Gold Dust Trails.* Santa Clara, Calif.: University of Santa Clara Press, 1946.

Wilson, Arlen Ray. "The Rock Springs, Wyoming, Chinese Massacre, 1885."
    Unpublished M.A. thesis, University of Wyoming, 1967.
Wong, Jade Snow. *Fifth Chinese Daughter*. New York: Harper, 1950.
Wynne, R. E. "Reaction to the .Chinese in the Pacific Northwest and British
    Columbia, 1850-1910." Unpublished Ph.D. dissertation, University of
    Washington, 1964.

SUPPLEMENTARY BIBLIOGRAPHY, 1972–91

THE "FURTHER BURGEONING" of Asian American studies predicted in 1972 has indeed taken place and to a degree no reasonable person could have imagined less than twenty years ago. The bibliography that follows is but a selection of the scholarly literature since then. Its focus is on the period before 1941; most works dealing with contemporary Chinese Americans and recent immigration of Chinese are ignored.

ROGER DANIELS

Armentrout-Ma, Eve. *Revolutionists, Monarchists and Chinatowns: Chinese Politics in the Americas and the 1911 Revolution.* Honolulu: University of Hawaii Press, 1990.

Beesley, David. "From Chinese to Chinese American: Chinese Women and Families in a Sierra Nevada Town." *California History,* 67 (1988): 168–179.

Carranco, Lynwood. "Chinese in Humboldt County, California: A Study in Prejudice." *Journal of the West,* 12 (1973): 139–162.

Chan, Loren B. "The Chinese in Nevada: An Historical Survey." *Nevada Historical Society Quarterly,* 25 (1982): 266–314.

Chan, Sucheng. *Asian Americans: An Interpretive History.* Boston: Twayne, 1991.

———, ed. *Entry Denied: Exclusion and the Chinese Community in America.* Philadelphia: Temple University Press, 1991.

———. "European and Asian Immigration into the United States in Comparative Perspective." In Virginia Yans-McLaughlin, ed., *Immigration Reconsidered: History, Sociology and Politics.* New York: Oxford University Press, 1990.

———, ed. *Social and Gender Boundaries in the United States: Studies of Asian, Black, Mexican and Native Americans.* Lewiston, N.Y.: Mellen, 1989.

———. *This Bittersweet Soil: The Chinese in California Agriculture, 1860–1910.* Berkeley and Los Angeles: University of California Press, 1986.

Chih, Ginger. *The History of Chinese Immigrant Women, 1850–1940.* North Bergen, N.J.: G. Chih, 1977.

Cohen, Lucy M. *Chinese in the Post–Civil War South: A People without a History.* Baton Rouge: Louisiana State University Press, 1984.

Cribbs, Lennie A. "The Memphis Chinese Labor Convention, 1869." *West Tennessee Historical Society Papers,* (1983): 176–183.

Crissman, Lawrence W. "The Segmentary Structure of Urban Overseas Chinese Communities," *Man,* n.s., 2 (1967): 185–204.

Daniels, Roger. "American Historians and East Asian Immigrants." *Pacific Historical Review,* 43 (1974): 448–472.

———, ed. *Anti-Chinese Violence in North America.* New York: Arno Press, 1978.

———. *Asian America: Chinese and Japanese in the United States since 1850.* Seattle: University of Washington Press, 1988.

———. "Chinese and Japanese in North America: The Canadian and American Experiences Compared." *Canadian Review of American Studies,* 17 (1986): 173–186.

Farrar, Nancy. *The Chinese in El Paso.* El Paso: Texas Western Press, 1972.

Fong, Lawrence M. "Sojourners and Settlers: The Chinese Experience in Arizona." *Journal of Arizona History,* 21 (1980): 227–256.

Fritz, Christian G. "Bitter Strength (*k'u li*) and the Constitution: The Chinese before the Federal Courts in California." *Historical Reporter,* 1 (1980): 2–15.

———. "A 19th Century 'Habeas Corpus Mill': The Chinese before the Federal Courts in California." *American Journal of Legal History,* 32 (1988): 347–372.

Glick, Clarence E. *Sojourners and Settlers: Chinese Migrants in Hawaii.* Honolulu: University of Hawaii Press, 1980.

Greenwood, Roberta S. "The Overseas Chinese at Home: Life in a 19th Century Chinatown in California." *Archaeology,* 31, no. 4 (1979): 42–49.

Hendrick, Irving R. *Public Policy toward the Education of Non-White Minority Group Children in California, 1849–1970.* Riverside: University of California, 1975.

Hirata, Lucie C. "Chinese Women in Nineteenth Century America." In Carol Berkin and Mary Beth Norton, eds., *Women of America: A History.* Boston: Houghton-Mifflin, 1979.

———. "Free, Indentured, Enslaved: Chinese Prostitutes in 19th Century America." *Signs,* 5 (1979): 3–29.

Kim, Hyung-chan. *Dictionary of Asian American History.* Westport, Conn.: Greenwood Press, 1986.

Kingston, Maxine Hong. *China Men.* New York: Alfred A. Knopf, 1980.

———. *The Woman Warrior.* New York: Alfred A. Knopf, 1976.

Kitano, Harry H. L., and Roger Daniels. *Asian Americans: Emerging Minorities.* Englewood Cliffs, N.J.: Prentice Hall, 1988.

Lai, Him Mark. "Island of Immortals: Chinese Immigration and the Angel Island Immigration Station." *California History,* 57 (1978): 88–103.

———, Genny Lim, and Judy Yung. *Island: Poetry and History of Chinese Immigrants on Angel Island, 1910–1940.* San Francisco: San Francisco Study Center, 1981.

Lee, Rose Hum. *The Growth and Decline of Chinese Communities in the Rocky Mountain Region.* New York: Arno Press, 1978.

Liestman, Daniel. "The Chinese in the Black Hills, 1876–1932." *Journal of the West,* 27, no. 1 (1988): 74–83.

Lim, Shirley Geok-lin et al., eds. *The Forbidden Stitch: An Asian American Women's Anthology.* Corvalis, Oreg.: Calyx Books, 1989.

Low, Victor. *The Unimpressible Race: A Century of Educational Struggle by the Chinese in San Francisco.* San Francisco: East/West, 1982.

Lyman, Stanford M. *Chinese Americans.* New York: Random House, 1974.

McClain, Charles J., Jr. "The Chinese Struggle for Civil Rights in America: The Unusual Case of *Baldwin v. Franks.*" *Law and History Review,* 3 (1985): 349–373.

———. "The Chinese Struggle for Civil Rights in Nineteenth Century America: The First Phase, 1850–1870." *California Law Review,* 72 (1984): 529–568.

McClain, Laurene Wu. "Donaldina Cameron: A Reappraisal." *Pacific Historian,* 27 (1983): 25–35.

McCunn, Ruthanne Lum. *Chinese American Portraits: Personal Histories, 1828–1988.* San Francisco: Chronicle, 1988.

McEvoy, Arthur F. *The Fisherman's Problem.* Cambridge: Cambridge University Press, 1987.

McKee, Delber L. "The Chinese Boycott of 1905–1906 Reconsidered: The Role of Chinese Americans." *Pacific Historical Review,* 55 (1986): 165–191.

———. *Chinese Exclusion versus the Open Door Policy, 1900–1906.* Detroit: Wayne State University Press, 1977.

———. "The Chinese Must Go! Commissioner General Powderly and Chinese Immigration, 1897–1902." *Pennsylvania History,* 44 (1977): 37–51.

Mann, Ralph. *After the Gold Rush: Society in Grass Valley and Nevada City, California, 1849–1870.* Stanford: Stanford University Press, 1982.

Mark, Diane Mei Lin, and Ginger Chih. *A Place Called Chinese America.* Dubuque, Iowa: Kendall/Hunt, 1982.

Martin, Mildred Crowl. *Chinatown's Angry Angel: The Story of Donaldina Cameron.* Palo Alto, Calif.: Pacific Books, 1977.

Mei, June. "Socioeconomic Origins of Emigration: Guangdong to California, 1850–1882." *Modern China*, 5 (1979): 463–501.

Nee, Victor G., and Brett de Bary Nee. *Longtime Californ': A Documentary Study of an American Chinatown.* New York: Pantheon Books, 1973.

Ng, Franklin. "The Sojourner, Return Migration, and Immigration History." In *Chinese America: History and Perspectives.* San Francisco: Chinese Historical Society, 1987.

Ong, Paul M. "The Central Pacific Railroad and the Exploitation of Chinese Labor." *Journal of Ethnic Studies*, 13 (1985): 119–124.

———. "An Ethnic Trade: The Chinese Laundries in Early California." *Journal of Ethnic Studies*, 8 (1981): 95–113.

Ourada, Patricia. "The Chinese in Colorado." *Colorado Magazine*, 29 (1952): 273–284.

Peffer, George Anthony. "Forbidden Families: Immigration Experiences of Chinese Women under the Page Law, 1875–1882." *Journal of American Ethnic History*, 6 (1986): 28–46.

Pozzetta, George E. "The Chinese Encounter with Florida, 1865–1920." In *Chinese America: History and Perspectives.* San Francisco: Chinese Historical Society, 1989.

Price, Charles A. *The Great White Walls Are Built: Restrictive Immigration to North America and Australia, 1836–1888.* Canberra: Australian National University Press, 1974.

Rhoades, Edward J. M. "The Chinese in Texas." *Southwestern Historical Quarterly*, 81 (1977): 1–36.

Riddle, Ronald. *Flying Dragons, Flowing Streams: Music in the Life of San Francisco's Chinese.* Westport, Conn.: Greenwood Press, 1983.

Rohe, Randall E. "After the Gold Rush: Chinese Mining in the Far West, 1850–1890." *Montana*, 12 (1982): 2–19.

Rusco, Mary. "Chinese in Lovelock, Nevada: History and Archaeology." *Halcyon*, (1981): 141–151.

Sayler, Lucy. "Captives of Law: Judicial Enforcement of the Chinese Exclusion Laws, 1891–1905." *Journal of American History*, 79 (1989): 91–117.

Schwendinger, Robert J. "Chinese Sailors: America's Invisible Merchant Marine." *California History*, 57 (1978): 58–69.

Shover, Michele. "Chico Women: Nemesis of a Rural Town's Anti-Chinese Campaigns, 1876–1888." *California History*, 67 (1988): 228–274.

Siu, Paul C. P. *The Chinese Laundryman.* New York: New York University Press, 1987.

Stockard, Janice. *Daughters of the Canton Delta, 1860–1930.* Stanford: Stanford University Press, 1989.

Stratton, David H. "The Snake River Massacre of Chinese Miners, 1887." In Duane A. Smith, ed., *A Taste of the West: Essays in Honor of Robert G. Athearn.* Boulder, Colo.: Pruett, 1983.

Takaki, Ronald. *Strangers from a Different Shore: A History of Asian Americans.* Boston: Little, Brown, 1989.

Tang, Vincent. "Chinese Women Immigrants and the Two-edged Sword of Habeas Corpus." In Genny Lim, ed., *The Chinese American Experience.* San Francisco: Chinese Historical Society, 1984.

Tipton, Gary P. "Men Out of China: Origins of the Chinese Colony in Phoenix." *Journal of Arizona History*, 18 (1977): 341–356.

Tsai, Shih-shan Henry. *China and the Overseas Chinese in the United States, 1868–1911.* Fayetteville: University of Arkansas Press, 1983.

———. *The Chinese Experience in America.* Bloomington: Indiana University Press, 1986.

Ueda, Reed. "The Coolie and the Model Minority: Reconstructing Asian-American History." *Journal of Interdisciplinary History,* 20 (1989): 117–24.

Wang, L. Ling-Chi. "The Yee Version of Poems from the Chinese Immigrant Station." *Asian American Review,* (1976): 117–126.

Wilson, Carol Green. *Chinatown Quest.* rev. 2d ed. San Francisco: California Historical Society, 1974.

Wong, Charles Choy. "The Continuity of Chinese Grocers in Southern California." *Journal of Ethnic Studies,* 8 (1980): 63–82.

Wong, Jade Snow. *No Chinese Stranger.* New York: Harper & Row, 1975.

Woon, Yuen-fong. "The Voluntary Sojourner among the Overseas Chinese: Myth and Reality." *Pacific Affairs,* 56 (1983/84): 673–690.

Wunder, John R. "The Chinese and the Courts in the Pacific Northwest: Justice Denied." *Pacific Historical Review,* 52 (1983): 191–211.

———. "Chinese in Trouble: Criminal Law and Race on the Trans-Mississippi Frontier." *Western Historical Quarterly,* 17 (1986): 25–41.

———. "The Courts and the Chinese in Frontier Iowa." *Idaho Yesterdays,* 25, no. 1 (1981): 21–32.

———. "Law and the Chinese in Frontier Montana." *Montana,* 30, no. 3 (1980): 18–31.

Yap, Stacy G. H. *Gather Your Strength, Sisters: The Emerging Role of Chinese Women Community Workers.* New York: AMS Press, 1989.

Yu, Connie Young. "The Chinese in American Courts." *Bulletin of Concerned Asian Scholars,* 4 (1972): 22–30.

———. "Rediscovered Voices: Chinese Immigrants and Angel Island." *Amerasia Journal,* 4, no. 2 (1977): 123–139.

Yung, Judy. "A Bowlful of Tears: Chinese Women Immigrants on Angel Island." *Frontiers,* 2 (1977): 52–55.

———. *Chinese Women of America.* Seattle: University of Washington Press, 1986.

———. "The Social Awakening of Chinese-American Women as Reported in Chung Sai Yat Po, 1900–1911." In Ellen Dubois and Vicki Ruiz, eds., *Unequal Sisters: A Multi-Cultural Reader in U.S. Women's History.* New York: Routledge, 1990.

Zo, Kil Young. "Chinese Emigration: The Means of Obtaining Passage to America." *Journal of Asiatic Studies,* 18 (1975): 215–230.

———. *Chinese Immigration to the United States, 1850–1880.* New York: Arno Press, 1978.

———. "Credit Ticket System for the Chinese Emigration into the United States." *Journal of the Nanyang University,* 8/9 (1974–75): 129–139.

INDEX